CATALYST

CATALYST

LEADERSHIP AND STRATEGY
IN A CHANGING WORLD

JOSEPH KOPSER & BRET BOYD

GRAYLINE
PUBLISHING

CATALYST

Leadership and Strategy in a Changing World

ISBN   978-1-5445-1015-6 *Paperback*

978-1-5445-1014-9 *Ebook*

CONTENTS

FOREWORD

Humanity is entering a fascinating period of world history in which we will experience more transformational global changes in a shorter time than ever before. We are on the cusp of several significant technological and socioeconomic shifts that have been building for decades. The success of our companies and public institutions will be the result of our ability to anticipate and react to these changes. As leaders, our organizations cannot thrive, and in some cases survive, if we ignore the changing environment and bury our heads in the sand, which as we will see is an all-too-common response.

We have titled this book *Catalyst* for two reasons. First, that is what we call the framework we have developed to help us sort the signal from the noise and identify truly transformational developments amid the sea of announcements we see in the media. A catalyst is a unique change—a transformational change—that alters the fundamental structures and global systems on which we build our industries, societies, and governments.

The second reason for the book's title is that we see leaders as catalysts themselves. Leaders drive change within organizations. Companies and public institutions do not transform themselves. Transformation requires people with the vision and courage to do things differently. Leaders are present in organizations at all levels—not just among CEOs, generals, and governors. Regardless of titles or formal responsibilities, leaders who serve as catalysts have the intrepidity to act, stepping off the path of least resistance in order to do what's right for their organizations.

By the end of this book, you should be able to identify some of the key transformations we believe are emerging—the technological and socioeconomic *catalysts*. We also hope to give you a framework to identify and evaluate the magnitude of new developments that will inevitably continue to emerge. Our intent is not to be 100 percent correct in our predictions, as these are complex and difficult issues with uncertain outcomes. If our predictions turn out to be completely accurate, it will likely mean that we have not thought far enough ahead. We simply seek to identify opportunities to inform your thinking, so that you can be better prepared to watch for, plan for, and respond to the emerging transformations that will impact your organization, community, and life.

INTRODUCTION

What will the world be like in a hundred years?

The world's oldest person, as of our writing this book in mid-2017, was a 117-year-old Jamaican woman named Violet Brown. While Ms. Brown passed away in late 2017, the changes she has witnessed during her lifetime are amazing to reflect on. At the time of her birth in spring 1900, the British Empire ruled the world, the second industrial revolution had kicked into high gear as capitalism expanded across the planet, and female suffrage in the United States was still just a dream. When she was born, homes with electricity, indoor plumbing, and telephones were rare. She lived to see a world where around one-third of the global population has a pocket-sized mobile computer (smartphone) connected to a global network of information and people (the internet).[1]

There is no question that in the 117 years of Violet Brown's life, she has experienced radical change. Almost every technological marvel we take for granted saw its breakthrough during her time on this planet; moreover, those transformations far outpace the rate of change witnessed in any preceding century. The pace of change is accelerating. A child born today will experience more change, more rapidly across his or her lifetime than Violet Brown had throughout hers.

Take the birth of Joseph's youngest daughter, Piper. She was born in Fort Hood, Texas, in spring 2000. From the hospital, Joseph used his mobile flip phone and the ward's pay phone to call his family's closest relatives to inform them of the news. Most of his relatives and friends would find out the news secondhand from those who were informed first. Now compare this to the scene a decade later, in summer 2010, when Bret's daughter Audrey was born. Thanks to smartphones and digital media, every friend and family member within their sphere had seen pictures of the latest addition to the Boyd family before mother and child left the hospital two days later.

If we were to compare Violet Brown's birth to that of another child born a decade later in 1910, we would have trouble distinguishing the two scenes. Advances in communication (radio) and transportation technology (automobile, flight) were emerging, but both families would have shared similar qualities of life and access to comparable amounts of knowledge. The difference between the birth scenes of our two daughters, even though also a decade apart, is far more significant. This is evidence of accelerating change, which will only continue.

THE POWER OF CATALYSTS

Change is constant, but not all change is equal. Some changes bring incremental improvements to current products or processes, and some changes affect absolutely *everything*. Incremental changes are interesting and important to businesses, but they do not cut across industries and geographies in the same fashion as more impactful transformations. These rarer and more impactful moments of change lead to fundamental transformations of the global system. We call these transformative changes *catalysts*.

Consider the widespread adoption of the personal computer: this catalyst transformed the lives of nearly every individual, business, and government organization in the world. New industries were created and old industries were destroyed as a result of the rise of this singular piece of technology.

Gordon Moore, the cofounder of Fairchild Semiconductor and Intel, famously articulated in 1965 that the increasing speed of transformation is a direct result of the exponential growth of computer power. His observation is commonly called Moore's law and posits that the number of transistors in an integrated circuit doubles every two years, leading to the exponential growth in processing power that the world has seen over the past fifty years.[2] The current pace of innovation continues to advance at this exponential rate, resulting in the more frequent arrival of new technologies that might serve as catalysts for future market shifts.

In hindsight, it makes sense that the emergence of the personal computer would lead to a whole new frontier of software applications—word processors, spreadsheets, accounting applications, and media players. At the time, however, many organizations remained skeptical of this catalyst's impact, or they misread how that impact would translate into new business opportunities and pressures. How could leaders know with confidence that there would be less of a need for personal assistants, traditional media, or centralized taxi companies—areas that had no apparent connection to core computing technology? Who could project that traditional aerospace and defense hardware companies, for example, would in many ways also become software companies? Yet Lockheed Martin's F-35 has evolved into a flying software platform with eight million lines of code.

Likewise, it would not have been natural to anticipate

the impact of the data analytics revolution on seismic modeling in the energy industry, nor the importance of computer imaging to the medical field, allowing doctors to repair internal organs through noninvasive procedures.

The second and third order effects of these transformations are extremely hard to anticipate, especially for organizations that are focused on the day-to-day efforts of running a business in highly competitive markets—a challenge that still very much exists for leaders today.

THE INCREASING PACE OF CHANGE

Catalysts that cause major market and social disruptions are occurring more frequently as a result of both technology and globalization. At one time, transformation on these levels was a once-in-a-century occurrence. In the twentieth century, the pace accelerated to a once-in-a generation phenomenon. Then it became every few decades. Now, as a result of the computer and information revolution, the cycles are even shorter. Organizations must now operate with the expectation that some or all of the market fundamentals they rely on for their success will shift at some point in the near future.

The increase in the potential avenues of disruption is a direct result of globalization. Globalization is a connecting force; today's markets, supply chains, consumer preferences, and national economies are increasingly interconnected. Interconnectedness means there is now a greater potential for an idea, company, or technology coming from an adjacent industry to impact other non-related or tangentially related industries. Many of these impacts are positive (computer modeling to increase crop yields), but others are not (iPhone's impact on the flash-light business).

In previous generations, companies and public institutions were more regionally and locally focused. With less global trade and without the connecting force of the internet, organizations had the luxury of primarily focusing on the dynamics of their local industry, customers, and competitors. In the age of globalization and interconnectedness, organizations must focus on not only disruptions in their own fields, but also other industries and regions of the world.

Metcalfe's law[3] states that the total value of a network is proportional to the square of the number of connected users of the system. Similarly, the network effect in economics describes the correlation between the value and size of a network. There is little question that businesses and consumers have benefited from the great growth that interconnected markets provide. Pre-globalization, a company could rise to the top if it was the only player in the region that could provide its particular service to consumers. As technology broke down those barriers, though, the natural monopoly of companies was suddenly threatened.

Take, for instance, a traditional farming company that has historically bought and sold produce in local US markets. In this new world, the company's leaders must keep a traditional focus on the competition, but they must also pay attention to advancements in modeling software development, genomic technologies, drones, sensors, and robotics—all while monitoring the Chinese and Brazilian economies, because they impact pricing, shipping costs, and the ability of nontraditional competitors in different regions to enter the market. The companies that stood still and hoped these dynamics would not impact their business are likely gone, or severely diminished. We have entered a new era that is only going to get more complex moving forward.

Leaders have the threefold challenge—they must identify the transformation (ideally before their peers), calibrate the correct response, and then implement the strategy inherent in that response. All three of these elements are difficult, and the far-reaching ripple effects of catalysts make these moments particularly challenging for leaders thinking about how to orient in preparation for an uncertain and rapidly changing future environment.

PROACTIVE VERSUS REACTIVE LEADERSHIP

Describing and identifying catalysts is not our only goal with this book. We also want to highlight the responsibility of leaders to act as catalysts within their own organizations.

Again, the responsibilities of leadership are not limited to CEOs and business owners. Any person at any level of an organization can step forward and help lead the organization into the future. Successful environments are ones where people act with the courage of their convictions, even (or especially) when their name is not emblazoned on the firm's door.

As leaders, we all need to think about how to position our organizations to survive and, hopefully, thrive in the face of these changes. Failing to correctly identify or react to a significant change could relegate your organization to a footnote in history, or a business-school case study about missed opportunities. Before we are able to make decisions about strategy and transformation, we need to correctly identify whether or not something important is happening, which is not an easy task in the current environment.

The media constantly bombards us with news stories about new research and startups positioned to upend entire industries. It is easy to assume cataclysmic changes are around every corner. However, most of these developments are white noise. It is increasingly important that we gain the skill and organizational discipline to focus on the sounds that matter.

Inside any organization, asking the right questions is a difficult balancing act. It falls on leaders to ask how and whether the items we perceive as noise are changing the assumptions that our strategy is built on.

If you are a senior executive at a furniture company, it is incumbent upon you to pause and reflect when your thirteen-year-old child spends his time walking around the neighborhood with his friends, bumping into trees as they play an augmented-reality game such as Pokémon GO. You notice that the game has hundreds of millions of downloads. It is up to you to determine whether this represents a passing trend or an indication of the potential importance of augmented reality, which could quickly evolve from a gaming tool to an important force that could reshape the retail experience. On the other hand, it might not reflect the emergence of a catalyst at all, in which case you will have wasted your time reacting, while a greater threat evolves in a different field. Although we will argue later in this book that augmented reality represents an important transformation, nobody has a crystal ball when it comes to properly identifying these changes.

Transforming an organization in response to changing market conditions is also extremely challenging, especially for large organizations. All businesses are people businesses. Leaders must be strategic but also be in tune with the day-to-day concerns and anxieties of the members of the organization as he or she charts the new course. To paraphrase General Dwight D. Eisenhower: A leader must stay far enough in front to provide the vision and direction, but not so far out front that the leader loses a personal connection to the group. Leaders who spend their days too far distanced from the core business may miss the implication of innovation to the detriment of their organizations.

PLANNING FOR THE FUTURE

Humans are generally not very good at predicting the future. We tend to anticipate a future environment that looks similar to the ways we now live but with extensions of current technologies—more apps, faster cars, better smartphones, and so forth. Large companies, in particular, have a terrible track record of anticipating and proactively positioning for significant market shifts.

History demonstrates that diminishment or failure is the most likely outcome for companies in markets that are disrupted by technological or socioeconomic shifts. For example, 88 percent of the *Fortune* 500 companies in 1955 were off the list by 2015.[4] The average life span of an S&P 500 company decreased from sixty-one years in 1958 to twenty-five years in 1980 to just fifteen years in 2012. In 2015, twenty-eight companies entered and left the S&P 500, reflecting a 5.6 percent churn rate. On average, an S&P 500 company is replaced every two weeks.[5]

The human predisposition to anticipate more familiarity and less change than what will actually occur is the major driver behind these failures. Some companies fail because their core assets are no longer valuable, leaving them with no options to react. More often, companies have options but lose market value or go out of business because the people who lead the organizations fail to acknowledge or make the difficult decisions often necessary to adapt to changing market conditions. People tend to be risk-averse; risk aversion is hardwired into our biology. We flee from uncomfortable, uncertain situations. Organizations often magnify this tendency with incentives and structures that further entrench the individual's sense of self-preservation.

With the obvious benefit of hindsight, let us highlight some of the woefully incorrect predictions made in response to emerging change by leaders who were ideally positioned to understand the impact of what was happening around them:

Thomas Watson, the president of IBM, said in 1943, "I think there is a world market for maybe five computers."[6]

As late as 1977, Ken Olsen, founder of Digital Equipment Corporation, said, "There is no reason anyone would want a computer in their home."[7]

In 1946, Darryl Zanuck, an executive at 20th Century Fox, said, "Television won't be able to hold on to any market it captures after the first six months. People will soon get tired of staring at a plywood box every night."[8]

In 2008, Blockbuster's CEO, Jim Keyes, said, "Neither Redbox nor Netflix are even on the radar screen in terms of competition. It's more Wal-Mart and Apple."[9]

In 1876, after having the chance to purchase the patent on Alexander Graham Bell's telephone, William Orton, president of Western Union, said, "What use could this company make of an electrical toy?"

Steve Ballmer, CEO of Microsoft, made this comment: "Google's not a real company. It's a house of cards."

The point of these quotes is not to poke fun at executives. Their comments merely demonstrate how difficult it is to identify industry disruptions, even for experts who are in the trenches leading successful business in industries that are being reformed by catalysts.

Sometimes companies identify and go as far as preparing for the disruption but are unable to pull away from their current strategy when it comes time to make the transition. Walter Isaacson, in his book *The Innovators*,[10] lays out how Kodak had invented the early technology of the digital camera and even went as far as securing the patents. They had all the keys to the next generation of this digital technology, but they refused to see how the developments in their industry were a threat to their core business: providing the chemicals needed to develop film. Kodak's missed opportunity to be ahead of the curve meant other companies beat them to the market and claimed their places as leaders. Kodak thought they were in the chemical business to make money developing pictures, when, in reality, they should have thought of themselves as being in the *memory* business.

Apple, on the other hand, kept their focus on what was through the windshield, rather than what was in the rearview mirror. They saw processors shrinking in size and increasing in capabilities, and recognized that the iPod would soon be outdated. Although the iPod generated more than 28 percent of Apple's revenue at the time,[11] it was nothing more than a single-use electronic device. Apple made the bold choice to deliberately cannibalize the iPod, the cornerstone of their business in order to create the iPhone. This self-inflicted disruption enabled Apple to grow into the most valuable company in the world.

Building the iPhone meant rewriting the job descriptions of a large part of the company in support of the new effort. Internal pushback when launching such an effort is inevitable, especially when incentives are not wholly aligned toward the transformation. Yet the leaders of this change persevered. There are numerous biases preventing organizations from correctly identifying the coming change and the steps needed to transform, but change is not impossible.

THIS IS NOT JUST ABOUT BUSINESS

We often think about market changes in terms of their impact on businesses: which companies will thrive and which will founder. However, catalysts and change management are not just business issues. Public organizations at the community, city, regional, and national levels must also innovate in response to a rapidly changing environment, which equally tests the leadership skills of all government employees, whether the person is a mayor, police officer, city worker, or federal agent.

Services fall behind when governments fail to keep up with changing technological possibilities and socioeconomic realities. At times, this falls within the bounds of acceptability; for example, continuing to deliver social security checks through standard mail instead of delivering them electronically will not adversely impact citizens in a material fashion, even if the process is not as efficient as it could be. Conversely, there are other areas, such as defense and public health, where a government that fails to innovate—going for long periods without adopting smarter practices—leads to major consequences in which citizens will suffer.

A prime example of this phenomenon can be seen in the United States with its gasoline tax. Many of the infrastructure problems that the United States experiences today are connected to the original design of the gas tax as a "use" tax, meaning vehicles on the road pay for the driving infrastructure they use. The more gas the vehicle operators utilize, the more money they contribute to the government's coffers, which is intended to fund infrastructure support. Meanwhile, environmental concerns have led to laws mandating fuel-efficient cars, which use less gas per mile of travel. In addition, government has incentivized car manufacturers to develop technologies that reduce gas consumption in order to reduce carbon emissions. All of this adds up to drivers using less gasoline per mile, which results in fewer tax dollars and less money for infrastructure. Concurrently, the costs of infrastructure development and repair are increasing.

As a result of this and other factors, American infrastructure has degraded to the point where it is considered to be woefully deficient in many areas. A use tax can be an excellent policy, but when it fails to achieve its stated purpose because of improvements in technology, government must adapt. We do not live in a world where public leaders can leave laws and regulations on the books for decades without reevaluating whether they still achieve their desired effects.

Emerging catalysts create opportunities for us to embrace change, reorienting our people and organizations to ensure we are equipped with the skills and capabilities necessary to compete in the emerging landscape. The purpose of this book is to help leaders think both about managing risk and identifying—then seizing—opportunity during these periods of transition.

Among the catalysts we will examine are the forces changing cities, demographics, manufacturing, power, and technology. We believe all of these issues are important to understand, regardless of what industry or public sector you support professionally. It is our hope that after reading this book, leaders will better understand the magnitude and speed of change that we will experience in the near future. Understanding facilitates action, and correct actions create better companies and public institutions that benefit us all.

WHO ARE WE?

We are Joseph Kopser and Bret Boyd, and we cofounded

the Grayline Group, a firm that helps companies and public institutions navigate the increasing pace of global change.

JOSEPH'S STORY

At every stage in life, whether as a teenager involved in student organizations or as an aerospace engineer at West Point, I have made it my mission to solve problems when I encounter them. I often bring a unique approach that comes from a blend of life experiences that allows me to see solutions in a new way.

At West Point, where I earned a BS in aerospace engineering, my approach to problem solving appeared in my senior thesis design. Combining emerging technologies with off-the-shelf concepts from other sectors, I designed a tank-carrying glider to answer an on-the-ground need to deliver superheavy military equipment more effectively. The project won the MIT Martin Marietta Engineering Competition, not because of the innovativeness or the project's content but because of my ability to explain the problem and my novel solution to the judges.

As a soldier in Iraq—part of a twenty-year military career during which I earned the Combat Action Badge, Army Ranger Tab, and Bronze Star—I continued to tackle difficult problems. For instance, I spent much of my time during my fourteen-month deployment fighting the bureaucracy to figure out how I could authorize EOD (Explosive Ordnance Disposal) bonuses—usually reserved only for bomb specialists—for the unit's engineers in the field. Day in and day out, these soldiers exposed themselves to IEDs (improvised explosive devices). By the end of my unit's combat tour, I had devised a way for all of them to receive hazardous-duty back pay. In this instance, I found a solution to an outdated set of regulations governing pay for a bygone era of warfighting.

In 2013, I cofounded the Defense Energy Summit to help the military improve their acquisition process in the areas of clean energy, cybersecurity, and defense innovation systems—essentially, it was a forum designed to help the military use the latest technologies to solve some of their greatest challenges. Its goal was to enable warfighters with the most innovative equipment in a more rapid manner than the older method of government procurement allowed.

The common thread running through my career is a pattern of constantly being pulled up to the next-highest level of headquarters to help with day-to-day challenges. After returning from Iraq the second time, for instance, I settled into a desk job, working with a staff focused on building the future force of the army. The general in charge took notice of my unique approach to problem solving and brought me in as a member of his personal staff. A year later, my work resonated with people inside the Pentagon, owing to my capacity to be comfortable with both military leaders and civilian leadership across the river on Capitol Hill.

While working in Washington, DC, I gained insight into the difficulty of making decisions regarding change of scale. There are, after all, few organizations in the world larger than the US military. I also witnessed the challenges of strategic leadership at the level of our nation's most senior leaders, working directly for General George Casey, the army chief of staff at the time.

As I moved into the private sector, I identified a coming catalyst and acted. I cofounded and became the CEO of RideScout, a Texas-based technology company that attempted to improve the daily lives of commuters by taking advantage of the changes happening in urban mobility. Executives at Mercedes-Benz picked up on the same trends and the work of RideScout. Again, I was pulled into a higher level of an organization when Mercedes acquired my company.

As I traveled around the country selling the merits of RideScout to investors, trade organizations, and transportation groups, people would often approach me after my talks to tell me how they had thought up an almost identical idea at one time, which is the truth about most great companies and ideas. Plenty of people and organizations do come up with the same ideas that end up changing businesses, industries, and the world. Execution, however, is a different beast altogether. My mission is to see ideas through to completion by building teams and staying focused on the mission at hand.

BRET'S STORY

I have had the privilege of working with senior leaders in a variety of industries and government organizations, providing a unique cross-sector view of how organizations develop and implement strategy.

In the course of helping build several different consulting and technology companies, I have worked with clients in the energy, consumer products, aerospace, defense, information services, technology, transportation, logistics, and finance sectors. I am a student of the way industries and organizations function, make money, define priorities, implement strategy, and provide services for their customers, especially in the face of changing market conditions.

I am a four-tour Iraq veteran, having served within the Special Operations community as an infantry officer in the 75th Ranger Regiment. Besides having the opportunity and privilege to work with great people in difficult situations, this period in my life provided a bias toward action, teaching me the value of simplification and first principles analysis to rapidly diagnose complex problems to facilitate action.

OUR SHARED MISSION

In summer 2016, after a series of conversations over the course of several years, we recognized that many of the challenges we faced in our respective careers in the private and public sectors came down to one primary question:

Can we come up with a better framework to enable organizations to proactively think about change and transformation?

As there is abundant evidence that the rate of change is accelerating, this question becomes more critical than ever. Successful organizations have elevated themselves to the top of their industries because they are excellent at executing their core mission. Leaders of these organizations tend to be smart men and women who deeply understand their industries and are constantly aware of potential threats and opportunities. However, sustaining everyday success in highly competitive markets requires focus and dedication. In most organizations, this manifests as a deluge of meetings, emails, and decisions. Keeping their heads above water, in other words, is a daily struggle for most executives. When it comes to the allocation of resources and talent, organizations ultimately focus on the problems of *now*, often at the expense of *tomorrow's* success.

Regardless of overwhelming near-term pressures, organizations must thoughtfully evaluate the potential impacts of change from many diverse sources. What is machine learning and how will it impact the business? How will augmented reality change their industry? What does the transition toward smart cities mean for their customer base?

The purpose of the Grayline Group is to bring together experts, data, and solutions to help organizations work through these issues, because understanding when to act is often as important as knowing what to do. It is one thing to lift a car's hood and observe that the engine is smoking. The real challenge is determining if and when the vehicle is going to break down, deciding what to do about the problem, and talking to people who can help solve it. This is where we believe the Grayline Group and this book add value.

In these pages we will discuss how change works, how leaders can respond to and manage change, and the emerging changes that are critical for leaders to understand. We have identified major catalysts in the areas of cities, demographics, manufacturing, power, and technology. Through stories, examples, and insights gleaned from our work helping organizations prepare for change, we hope to help you see the coming catalysts as opportunities, not threats, so that your organizations can also become agents of change.

PART ONE

CHANGE

HOW CHANGE WORKS

Change occurs in steps—long periods of incremental improvement followed by short periods of transformation that results in a new paradigm. The specific frequency of these steps differs across industries, but it is universally true throughout all industries that the time between these steps is shrinking. Technology is the primary driver for this acceleration, and globalization has created an environment where the horizontal impacts of these paradigm shifts are broader than ever before. Historically, large organizations are not adept at predicting or adapting to transformational change.

Change does not occur in a linear fashion. When we map out the evolution of an industry, region, or social system, we do not see slow and steady progress with evenly spaced technological, geopolitical, and socioeconomic developments. Rather, we see that change moves in steps. We start with an existing paradigm, then experience a period of incremental improvements, followed by an extremely important period of condensed activity that results in a leap into a new paradigm.

The energy industry, for example, has evolved slowly over

time, but each shift has changed the world. Wind was the primary transportation energy source for thousands of years. The change in primary naval locomotion from sail to steam was so important and pervasive that it literally changed the map as lumber plantations were replaced by island coal depots as strategic outstations around the world. The transition from steam to oil occurred after around 150 years and similarly reshaped the strategic and economic map of the world as oil producers replaced coal mines and coaling stations in strategic importance. We are around a hundred years into the age of oil, and the maturation of solar, wind, and energy storage technologies leads us to believe that we are approaching the next paradigm shift in the energy industry, which could have as significant of a global impact as the transition from coal to oil.

Communications technology provides us with another example to illustrate how change moves in steps. The Pony Express operated in 1859, arguably representing the pinnacle of a long series of incremental improvements to letter-delivery technology. Seventeen years later, a patent for the telephone was issued to Alexander Graham Bell, which provided near-instantaneous, one-way delivery of messages and changed the world. Business, diplomacy, military strategy, and family life all changed when the world shifted from mail to telegraph. Incremental improvements over time led to better performance and wider adoption, and while these enhancements benefited people's lives, they did not upend industries until the next major inflection point—the telephone—which again transformed global economic and political systems.

CHANGE AS A STEP FUNCTION
KEY TECHNOLOGIES THAT CHANGED GLOBAL COMMUNICATIONS

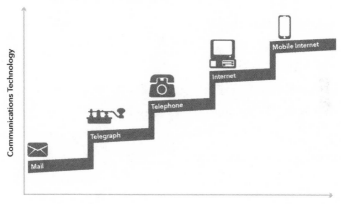

Conversely, many markets experience these transformations on far shorter timelines. The grocery business in the United States, for example, has shifted from farmers' markets, to the small-town grocery store, to the big-box supermarket, to the emerging blend of specialty plus online in the last one hundred years. Live media has similarly shifted from radio, to television, to online, to mobile. All markets evolve in shifts, albeit on different timelines. The inflection points that mark these shifts are extremely important for business and public sector leaders to understand.

SHORTENING CYCLES OF CHANGE

The pace of change is accelerating, which is shortening the cycle time between market shifts. This is happening for two primary reasons: technology and globalization.

The digital revolution, and, before that, the Industrial Revolution, created tools and systems that self-propagate, enabling faster and faster technological development. Generally speaking, existing technology has always provided the foundation for the next new generation of technologies. Computers have significantly accelerated this dynamic because, with computers, we have created not just a knowledge base to build on, but toolsets that accelerate the development of subsequent generations of technologies in all fields.

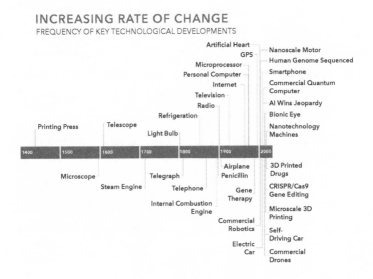

INCREASING RATE OF CHANGE
FREQUENCY OF KEY TECHNOLOGICAL DEVELOPMENTS

At its core, globalization is a movement toward more and more interconnectivity between markets. The greater the connection between peoples, countries, and global markets, the faster the diffusion of innovation through the global system.

Interconnected supply chains and globally specialized companies and, in some cases, countries have created a different environment than humanity has ever operated in. This provides great efficiencies for companies, as they are able to source components globally and sell into international markets. But while companies and nations share in the positive, global interconnectivity creates and magnifies risk. A disruption in one market has global spillover effects to an extent that had never before been possible. The financial crisis of 2008 provides us with a remarkable illustration of this truism, as a disruption to the American real estate market affected everything from Chinese manufacturing employment to worldwide oil prices.

GLOBAL CONNECTIVITY
REAL TRANSPORT AND COMMUNICATION COSTS, RELATIVE TO 1930

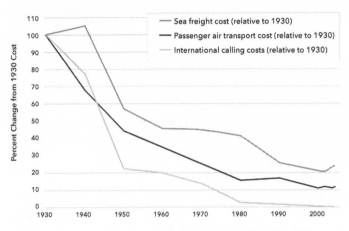

Source: Jean-Yves Huwart, and Loic Verdier, *Economic Globalism: Origins and Consequences* (OECD Publishing: Paris, 2013), http://dx.doi.org/10.1787/9789264111905-en.

There has always been change. Change itself is not what is different about the current world in which we live; it is the rate of change we now face that is a unique and unprecedented phenomenon. It is increasingly difficult for leaders today to project how the world, and by extension their industries, will evolve in the next decade. Leaders used to have the luxury of assuming general continuity within most industries for decades. Now, in an environment where business models are being disrupted more and more frequently, predicting even a few years into the future may prove futile, which significantly affects how organizations plan and implement strategy.

This is the dilemma leaders face: forward planning and

strategic agility is both more important and more difficult than ever before. However, despite the challenge, they must engage with and plan for change proactively. If they do not, they risk missing these market transitions entirely, which will cause their organizations to share the same fate as countless other companies and governments that failed to adapt in previous periods of transition.

There is no single industry, country, or region that will not change significantly in the next five-to-ten years. Organizations that believe they have the luxury of time and that change will never impact their way of life simply will not last long in the emerging world. Organizations have an imperative to evolve to match the pace of change of their surrounding environment. Strategic evolution is not a luxury that will differentiate the outstanding from the average performers in an industry; it is a matter of survival.

THE TRAP OF LINEAR FORECASTING

Humans are generally not very good at predicting how the future will look. The natural inclination is to anticipate the future through the bias of the present with advances that are enhancements of current systems and trends, rather than leaps of innovation to fundamentally new technologies and environments. A walk through Violet Brown's twentieth-century experience illustrates how different the future is from what is commonly envisioned.

Consider 1900, the year Violet Brown is born. The British Empire is the center of the universe. In fact, the worldwide system of time zones is centered in Greenwich, England. Great Britain launched the first and second industrial revolutions. The women's rights and suffrage movements are also emerging. And at the dawn of the twentieth century, it is that clear Violet has been born into an era of unparalleled peace and prosperity. Globalization and the economic interconnections that have been established in recent decades make the idea of war sound impossible and irrational. Ms. Brown's parents and their neighbors anticipate a continuation of the British century; they imagine the many awe-inspiring ways in which the world will develop. At the dinner table, they talk about the inventions of the day: electric lights making the whole city glow, men developing and testing the very first machines of flight, and the automobile, a fantastic luxury product for the wealthy. There is an air of excitement, forward progress, immense positivity, and optimism; the accelerating rate of change around the world is almost difficult to believe, and life feels increasingly like a joyride in the automobile so few, as of yet, are able to own.

Now jump to 1920. The future predictions from 1900 have proven to be fantastically incorrect. World War I has been a watershed global event, a catalyst that fundamentally changed the entire global system into something that is nearly unrecognizable. The modern technologies that had been so eagerly anticipated two decades before evolved into instruments of destruction to support the needs of the war. Industrial Revolution technologies applied to warfare have turned much of Western Europe into a pitted, smoldering wasteland; tanks, barbed wire, and machine guns transformed battlefields into what soldiers at the time called meat grinders; the machines of progress and innovation that earlier represented the boundless progress of humanity have found their primary use as instruments of horror and bloodshed.

Europe as it existed in 1900 is gone. Long-standing regimes across the continent have evaporated; the governmental and business landscape is a whole new frontier. In Britain, between 700,000 and one million people, or around 2 percent of the population, have been killed. The British Empire gained significant territory during the war, but the war's strain on resources has cost the empire its position as the world's preeminent military and industrial power. The decline of the British Empire has clearly begun, an evolution that no one would have predicted in 1900.

Still, there are hopeful signs for the future. Most observers—having witnessed Europe's self-immolation, the state of revolt of many European armies, and financial exhaustion—agree that a war of the great powers on such a massive scale will never happen again. And progress marches on, following an albeit altered path: car manufacturers assembling cars their workers can actually afford, and the very first radio stations receive broadcast licenses the following year. The common view in 1920 is that the costs were proven too high and there will never again be a large-scale war; they anticipated a future built around renewal and reconstruction.

Fast forward to 1940. The people of Europe despair as the German army sweeps across the continent, and the most common forecast was that Germany would win the war and rule Europe. The reconstruction effort following World War I did not progress as quickly as many anticipated and was accompanied by poverty, famine, and massive hyperinflation, leading to disenfranchisement and unrest. This has contributed to the rise of Hitler and Mussolini. A year into World War II, it seems clear to most observers that the world is entering the German era.

Welcome to 1960. Germany does not control Europe; in fact, it does not even exist as a country anymore. It has been split into two separate countries, in an arrangement that characterizes the world's current division. The threat of another Great War is enhanced by the new threat of a nuclear war. It is now clear that Great Britain's days of dominance are entirely over, but the United States, physically separated from much of the military action, has been spared from similar levels of destruction, outside of Pearl Harbor. Although large parts of Europe and the

Pacific were destroyed—with some fifty to eighty million casualties—the United States emerges in a position to rebuild and remake large parts of the world order.

Nevertheless, the country finds itself in a rivalry with the Soviet Union, the world's other superpower and a country that shares similar aims. The Soviets are equally innovative, and it appears that they will win the space race. Nuclear devastation is a real possibility, as military strategies are built on the principle of mutually assured destruction. The United States and the Soviet Union are engaged in conflict across the globe, from Latin America to Africa to Southeast Asia.

Back in the United States, the popularity of the home television set has ended the golden age of radio. Thanks to the GI Bill, the Federal-Aid Highway Act of 1956, and eminent domain laws, Americans are starting to move out of the cities into the suburbs. Future predictions are biased by the present ideal of virtuous nuclear American families, stay-at-home mothers, white picket fences, and strong conservative values. The United States has never been more economically powerful.

But on New Year's Day 1980, most people see the Soviets in prime position to emerge from the Cold War as the dominant power, with the United States still reeling from a socially and politically impactful, decade-long war in Southeast Asia. The election of Ronald Reagan means that the United States will continue to expand its military in an effort to oppose the Soviets, who have recently started a minor operation in Afghanistan. Radio has made a comeback thanks to the growth of call-in talk shows that allow listeners to interact with the hosts and guests. Deregulation in the airline industry has led to a significant drop in prices, resulting in tremendous growth in demand for airline travel. Millions of people who had never set foot on a plane are now regular air passengers. Personal computers appear in more and more homes, and young people—not guided by universities or corporations—start teaching themselves and each other how to program them.

Fast forward to 2000. The Soviet Union did not win the Cold War as seemed likely in 1980; it fell apart. With the collapse of the Soviet Union and the Eastern Bloc countries, the United States is the unquestioned world hegemon. The country has enjoyed a decade of explosive economic and industrial growth, and the current generation of young people has never known war. The dot-com boom and advancing internet technologies represent a limitless new landscape of progress and advancement.

No one's future predictions, at this moment in time, foresee a massive global political and economic shift twenty-one months later when terrorists hijack and fly two commercial jet liners into the World Trade Center.

The common theme of this anecdote is that the mainstream view of the future is generally wrong, even on a timeline as short as twenty years. In general, people do not imagine a world that is as utterly divergent from the current state, as is almost always the case. We tend to anticipate a future that looks like the present, with slight variations on existing themes. This predisposition leads us to underestimate how significant change will be. This becomes more and more important as the cycle time between major change shortens.

Leaders must both develop good strategy *and* have a correct understanding of the environment in which that strategy will operate. The best strategies will fail if they are built on assumptions that prove incorrect. In our experience, businesses and governmental groups tend to allocate large amounts of time, money, and personnel to strategy development, while dedicating few resources toward building a systemic understanding of the future operating environment. Organizations therefore tend to build three-, five-, or ten-year strategic plans using a future very similar to the present as their baseline projection. This approach, and the strategies it generates, is often flawed from the onset.

As we have discussed, the time between system-wide shifts is shrinking. The likelihood of being impacted by one of these shifts in the near term is high, and the likelihood of predicting them without a deliberate evaluation framework is low, given the built-in biases that prevent us from anticipating transformational change.

SOCIAL IMPACTS OF CHANGE

Technology can disrupt the foundation of not only business and national strategy but also society's institutions and norms. It took the widespread use of photography for people to understand the carnage of the Civil War and the deep implications of the savagery of slavery. Photographers such as Sojourner Truth used still images distributed on postcards as fuel for the fire of the antislavery sentiment that helped ignite the Civil War.[12]

Later, radio, which provided a cheap and efficient way to communicate with large groups of people, played a similarly important role in the history of social movements, such as women's suffrage and the organization of unions. More recently, Twitter and other social media tools have been regarded as important enablers of the 2010–2012 so-called Arab Spring.

Put simply, some technologies change the dynamics of interaction between people. Our social, educational, and governmental structures are built around the way people work and interact. When technology changes, these structures also need to change. Unfortunately, social structures now take longer to evolve than technology, and the gap is widening.

For thousands of years, men and women have inhabited culturally defined roles based on gender. This is how most societies were structured until the last one to two generations. Several technological and socioeconomic shifts occurred over the past fifty years that resulted in women moving into the workforce in significant numbers.

The positives of this development are obvious. An extraordinary amount of human capital was unleashed as women moved into the workforce and new roles in society. This has enabled an explosion of capacity and productivity in both the public and private sectors. Still, there are some second and third order effects that have not been fully addressed to this day, such as fair pay and benefits for women, high divorce rates, more children raised in daycare, and the breakdown in the "traditional" family structure. We still have work to do in order to reshape our social institutions to adjust to the revolution that happened more than half a century ago.

No more than thirty years ago, people needing a phone number had to look it up in the Yellow Pages. If their child was doing a report for school, they would pull out the encyclopedia, if they had a set at home. If not, they would have to travel to the local library. Now, smartphones allow people to have the entirety of the world's information in the palm of their hand. Although this is a benefit from an information and accessibility standpoint, it also carries a negative component. Technology applications are rapidly changing the way we interact with one another, and with our environment. Take the question of the impact of screen time on children, or the fact that while there is a lot of good information on the internet, there is also a lot of disinformation. We will continue to move on to newer technologies, such as embedded devices or contact lens overlays, which will raise new questions before we have fully incorporated the current technologies into our societal standards and structures.

The media is another area where this social dynamic plays out. At one time in the United States, most of the country gathered every night in front of the television to hear Walter Cronkite report on the day's events. Back then, people on all sides of political discourse viewed the same news and operated from a common base of information. There were disagreements, to be certain, but dialogue was enabled by a common set of "truths" from which people formed their different conclusions.

In contrast, today, media has transitioned from a public

service into a 24/7 entertainment business. There are many competing entertainment channels, each of which reports on different topics with different views selected to entertain their audience. People read papers and websites that conform to their existing views, from which there are thousands to choose. They lean into the echo chamber that validates their own opinions and perspectives. This means, ultimately, that people watching left- and right-leaning news networks operate based on different facts, making informed and civil debate deeply challenging—to the detriment of social cohesion.

The disruptions to our social structures that come as a result of this tension should neither lead us to pine for the past nor prevent us from celebrating progress. Contrary to nostalgic memories of the Walter Cronkite days, the media of yesterday was also all too capable of twisting facts to suit its needs and to a much greater degree.

A famous example is when newspaper magnate William Randolph Hearst sent a journalist to Cuba to report on the Spanish-American War. The reporter sent back word that no such war existed.

Hearst told the reporter, "You furnish the pictures, and I'll furnish the war."[13]

The difficulties we currently experience do not indicate

that we should regress toward the past; rather, they signal our need for time, space, and ingenuity to allow social structures to catch up to the rapid changes. Ignoring the social impacts of rapidly changing technology is a high-risk proposition.

THE POLITICAL IMPACTS OF CHANGE

Similarly, there are very real political impacts of change that we must also consider. History teaches us that governments risk disaster if they fail to adapt to changing conditions—whether those are technological, social, or geopolitical. The political systems that have managed to evolve in the face of change provide lessons for leaders of all different types of organizations.

The founders of the United States, in an effort to come up with a political system that could endure where all others have failed, studied the history of government startups—such as Ancient Greece and the Roman Empire—experimented with town halls and representative systems, and incorporated Enlightenment-era philosophy. What resulted was the United States Constitution, a new type of governance system. The amendment system within the Constitution meant it was a living document, an acknowledgment that they did not have a perfect system and needed the ability to innovate as they continued to grow and meet new challenges.

How much easier it would be for companies to innovate if they built a framework from the beginning designed to evolve and adapt with the environment as that environment inevitably changes. A structure would be in place to reevaluate key institutions and operating principles as the environment changed, much the same way the United States Constitution has been able to respond to the myriad of significant changes it has been forced to adapt to in its history—from changing economic models (agrarian to industrial to digital) to social institutions (slavery and women's rights) to macroeconomic and geopolitical forces (from the Great Depression to the Cold War).

SEEING THE OPPORTUNITY IN THE THREAT

Change creates both risk and opportunity. Winners and losers alike emerge from market shifts. We can look at the data and find reasons to despair, or we can envision how these changes create new possibilities and opportunities.

Life expectancy is now longer than it has ever been in human history. Innovations made by businesses, governments, and academia have succeeded in suppressing violence and sickness in the world compared to earlier generations. We not only live longer, but our quality of life is also higher. This means hundreds of millions of people are now creating demand for air-conditioning, refrigeration, television, and internet access. The challenge for us is to continue improving lives without leaving people behind.

In 1942, Joseph Schumpeter coined the term *creative destruction* to describe "the process of industrial mutation that incessantly revolutionizes the economic structure from within, incessantly destroying the old one, incessantly creating a new one."[14] In other words, companies create new opportunities through better business models, tools, products, and services that eat away at the original foundation that built the company's success. It is a difficult but healthy process. As we get smarter about using human labor and physical capital more efficiently, it frees up our resources and allows us to create. In a certain sense, the people who lose their jobs can take their knowledge in a particular industry or discipline and either find better work or create other companies related to their skills.

Regardless of whether the catalysts that we will discuss in detail manifest themselves as a threat or opportunity to your specific organization, one thing is clear: ignoring the inevitably of change is not a winning strategy.

CHANGE MANAGEMENT AND LEADERSHIP

Most successful organizations are built around efficiency, which leads to structures that inhibit agility in the face of significant technological or socioeconomic change. The normal trajectory for a successful company that reaches the top of an industry is to be significantly diminished or destroyed when fundamental market conditions shift. These challenges also apply to public sector and academic institutions.

By 2007, the US Army had implemented several new approaches to counter an increasingly challenging insurgency in Iraq, such as a program to establish more direct relationships with the local populations. The strategy, which proved successful in many parts of the country, decentralized the force, moved away from large bases, and recirculated the same US personnel into the same region each deployment. In September 2009, the military attempted a similar approach in Afghanistan, launching the Afghanistan-Pakistan (AfPak) Hands program. With this program, the military identified and trained personnel in the complexities of the language and culture of specific regions within Afghanistan and Pakistan. This coincided with smaller and more frequent rotations, enabling those military personnel to truly become experts and build continuity within their tour of duty.

Some leaders were hesitant to fully commit to this groundbreaking strategy because it deviated from their training and the established structure of the military. Strategically important decisions were being made in the field by officers and noncommissioned officers at lower and lower levels.

Problems arose because the program was not resourced the same throughout all branches of the military; different branches were not investing the same resources and priority. If institutional infrastructure does not align with the senior leaders' vision, disconnects will be created and will have long-term negative implications.

Existing leadership feared that the unorthodox nature of the program meant the military's institutions of promotion and assignment selection process would struggle to acknowledge these assignments when it came time for recognition and advancement.[15] Their concerns were later proved right: the officers involved were often overlooked for promotion, and the program was recently shut down. Rather than providing an *incentive*, the program became a *disincentive*.

In this example, senior leaders understood that they

needed to adjust strategy, and they took steps to implement something new. But, as it turns out, there is more involved in significant change management than leadership decisions—an entire organizational and institutional realignment is needed, and this can be extremely difficult to obtain, despite the best efforts of proactive leaders.

Too often, different levels within organizations have different priorities throughout their structures, which is an easy trap to fall into given the myriad problems present on a day-to-day basis. The argument is simple: you do not get to plan for the future if you do not succeed in the present, and the crush of the *now* is consuming.

Imagine a team of rowers closing in on the final three hundred meters of the race. The coxswain sits at the stern yelling at everyone to row, when suddenly one of the members starts to consider a different technique. He slows down to refine the new method, and it is quite obvious what happens next. The rest of the crew is yelling at him to pick up the pace. In a matter of seconds, this one person has thrown the entire team into disarray, creating tension and anxiety with his idea to move in a different direction. The race will be lost.

In an economy built around efficiency and a society that preaches the virtue of being a team player, organizations strive to become well-oiled machines. Companies and public institutions are optimized to execute tasks with the fewest people and lowest cost possible. Efficiency, however, comes with a cost and, in many cases, stands in opposition to adaptability. Organizationally rigid cultures tend to default to the status quo due to this alignment of financial and cultural incentives toward efficiency at the expense of innovation. Additionally, individuals tend not to make decisions out of alignment with their peers or company. Personal bias toward job safety causes people to "stick with the herd" until enough of their peers act; however, it is important to remember that the sense of safety is false, because in sticking with the herd, you are likely to realize too late that you are headed off the proverbial cliff.

Growth can only happen when leadership creates safe spaces for managed change. An old adage states that rules are for 95 percent of the people, 95 percent of the time, while innovation occurs in the remaining 5 percent of the time, among 5 percent of the population. Many examples of successful innovation and transformation are cases where leadership built structures to isolate and facilitate the success of that 5 percent.

When Xerox made the strategic decision to innovate in the digital space, it opened a research center in Palo Alto, California, across the country from its headquarters in Rochester, New York. The intention was to minimize interaction between the traditional structure and the innovation group, because each needed entirely different processes to support their objectives. They did not want their innovators to be too close to headquarters and risk being influenced by the day-to-day concerns. It is not that the day-to-day concerns are inherently worse than those of the innovation team, but they are simply different and were appropriately recognized as such.

For better or worse, shareholders and public markets tend to set short-term financial performance as the top priority. Incredibly, quarterly financial performance is often the only metric that investors value or even look at. CEOs of publicly traded companies understand this and are often compensated with stock that moves in response to those quarterly numbers. Understandably, these corporate leaders tend to direct the majority of resources—financial, personnel, and investment capital—toward the execution of those quarterly financial results. In many cases, this is healthy. Companies must execute routine business tasks in order to thrive. It becomes a problem when the focus on the now comes at the expense of the future, when long-term planning becomes a fringe activity rather than a driving force.

It makes sense from a near-term business perspective to have your best people and a majority of your resources focused on the issues of today, but that cannot come at the expense of a thoughtful, proactive long-term strategy.

CHARACTERISTICS OF ADAPTABLE ORGANIZATIONS

It is important to note that the normal course for an excellent company is to grow to a position of market leadership, endure for a while, and then fade into irrelevance once something happens that causes that company's market to shift. The evidence for this can be seen across the S&P 500, *Fortune* 500, and other metrics of market leadership.

Eighty-eight percent of the *Fortune* 500 companies from 1955 are no longer in existence. As the cycle time between market shifts shrinks, so does the time period when companies enjoy a position of market leadership. According to research conducted by Mark Perry of the University of Michigan, of the *Fortune* 500, 62.4 percent were replaced between 1995–2016, representing an average of 14.2 entrants per year, up from 8.5 new entrants per year from 1955–1994.[16]

MARKET LEADERSHIP TENURE
RAPID S&P 500 AND FORTUNE 500 TURNOVER HAS BECOME THE NORM

Average tenure of companies on the S&P 500 was 33 years in 1965, 20 years in 1990, and is forecast to shrink to 14 years by 2026.	62.4% of the Fortune 500 was replaced between 1995 and 2016, representing an average of 14.2 entrants per year, up from 8.5 between 1955 and 1994.

Source: Mark J. Perry, "Fortune 500 Firms 1955 vs. 2016," AEIdeas, December 2016, http://www.aei.org/publication/fortune-500-firms-1955-v-2016-only-12-remain-thanks-to-the-creative-destruction-that-fuels-economic-prosperity/.

"Creative Destruction Whips through Corporate America," S&P 500 Lifespans Are Shrinking, Innosight, accessed January 22, 2018, https://www.innosight.com/insight/creative-destruction-whips-through-corporate-america-an-innosight-executive-briefing-on-corporate-strategy/.

These statistics illustrate the challenge that even the most successful companies have in adapting to changing market conditions that result from technological or socioeconomic shifts. No doubt those companies were considered giants of their day, perhaps even untouchable and immune to market shifts. We almost take it for granted that the FANG companies—Facebook, Amazon, Netflix, Google—and other titans of today are in a prime position to maintain their positions as industry leaders for the next sixty-plus years. While these organizations are worth studying, it is important to note at the onset of this discussion that they are not immune to risk. In fact, if history is any guide, we would expect one or more of these companies to be significantly diminished within ten years. We have yet to see a company that maintained market dominance indefinitely.

In 1998, Google's original mission statement was "to organize the world's information and make it universally accessible and useful."[17] What is compelling about this mission is its acknowledgment that the search engine is not an end in itself; rather, Google saw it as a means to an end. The service—accessibility and usefulness—was as important as the product—information. Google has maintained its position at the leading edge of innovation in part because early on, in an effort to realize their mission, they put an emphasis on hiring people who brought curiosity to their work and would take an expansive view of the mission. Once the company built a reputation for having an innovative workforce, it became easier to attract innovative people who operate well in this environment of constant transformation.

Google's leaders have been willing to experiment, a critical component of adaptability. Before expanding into the technological empire that is Alphabet, Inc., Google attempted several billion-dollar investments that subsequently failed. Google Answers, Google Catalog Search, Google Web Accelerator, iGoogle, Google Reader, and Google Lively are just some of the company's massively funded product fails. Yet the company never allowed these disappointments to stymie its innovative approach.

Google is not alone in this willingness to fail. The United States, in fact, produces Unicorns—startups valued at more than $1 billion—at a much faster rate than Europe, primarily because of a business and regulatory culture that facilitate innovation by not prohibitively punishing failure. There has been a remarkable amount of failure to produce these incredible successes—more than 90 percent of startups fail. Failure, in a certain sense, is seen in the United States as the learning experience it is, as opposed to a mark of shame. The key is to make sure those involved correctly identify and learn from their mistakes.

While the technology wave has carried the FANG companies through exponential growth, these companies have yet to face an existential market shift. When a new entrant comes in and upends an industry, they displace jobs, impact profit margins, and eliminate previously existing areas of commercial opportunity. They also create new opportunities, but many of these opportunities are not business lines that the incumbents can service. Not even the FANG companies are immune from this possibility, which should cause any business leader trying to manage a large organization to sit up and pay attention to emerging areas of change. The challenge for large companies during times of transformation is to balance the best qualities that enabled their success with the requirement created by the new market conditions. This transition is not impossible, but, in many cases, it is more difficult for the incumbents to adapt than it is for the new entities who have the benefit of starting from a blank sheet of paper.

BUSINESSES WITH RESILIENCY

We tend to think of technology companies when we think of agile organizations, but technology companies are not the only types of organizations that can innovate.

The American oil and gas industry, for example, while not typically thought of in this way, has actually proven to be extremely agile and adaptive. This is an industry where boom and busts come rapidly and dramatically in the form of fluctuating oil prices, so companies have learned how to manage their ups and downs. Considering the volatility of the industry, it is interesting to note that most of the current owners and leaders in oil and gas are second- or third-generation descendants of wildcatters, the industry's original pioneers—meaning they have weathered volatility through decades of generational adaptation.

Wildcatters got their start in the industry by scraping together money to buy up land leases and secure property and mineral rights, especially in places such as Pennsylvania and Texas. Many times, these entrepreneurs would drill holes across a leased property and come up with nothing but dirt, rendering the investment worthless. Failing to find oil often meant bankruptcy. Even so, the next day, they would be out looking for new investors, selling them on discovered geological features that may eventually yield oil.

More than a century later, wildcatter DNA lives on in these companies. Modern oil and gas exploration companies are highly sophisticated at the risk and capital management practices required in exploration for hydrocarbons, and historically, they have demonstrated a willingness to change strategies quickly when an investment proves nonproductive. The industry has evolved into a complex network of capital partners and hedging strategies that allow these companies to place large exploration bets in a thoughtful and risk-managed fashion.

This sense of agility flows through the strategies of many of these companies, as they have capitalized their businesses in such a fashion that allows them to divest assets and cut costs quickly as the need arises. Exploration and production companies can scale up and down with surprising maneuverability for their size, and they are keenly aware of the steps they need to take in order to survive. It remains to be seen whether this agility will translate into adaptability in the face of a transformational technological shift, which may be emerging as renewable technologies mature.

Energy utilities, on the other hand, are not known for their agility, in part because of their heritage in operating as a heavily regulated industry. Generally speaking, utility companies generate their greatest profits when customer usage is at its height. They benefit from increased energy and resource consumption and, conversely, suffer a financial disincentive when their customers use more energy-efficient systems that require less electricity.

Michael Webber, an energy expert at the University of Texas at Austin, envisions a major shift coming to this sector. He envisages utilities that view energy as a service rather than a product piped into homes. In this new model, companies could receive a monthly fee, meaning they would make more money when consumers cut down on energy consumption. With this kind of incentive to reduce the electricity bills of customers, utilities would work to get energy-efficient appliances into customers' hands through leasing or other similar programs. They could also partner or vertically integrate with construction companies to build more energy-efficient homes, or with solar companies to facilitate solar panel installation. It is also possible to imagine a scenario where consumers lease or finance more energy-efficient products such as refrigerators and air-conditioning units with the help of the utility company, because both sides would benefit from lower energy consumption.

This novel business model is not the only transformation facing energy utility companies. The convergence of technologies in the fields of power generation, energy distribution, electrical grids, grid storage batteries, energy monitoring sensors, and thermostat systems will drive a shift in the way this industry works. Unfortunately, due in part to regulatory requirements, many traditional energy utilities are not putting forward the effort to reinvent their organizations to meet the potential of these new technologies and business models. They are still unwilling to take the risk of destroying the old, still-profitable structures.

In other industries, companies have transformed their organizations in response to changing market conditions in their own ways. For example, Nestlé, one of the largest packaged food companies in the world, was originally focused on selling less-than-healthy foods such as cookies, candies, and chocolates. In 1997, in the early days of the trend toward more health-conscious eating, their CEO, Peter Brabeck-Letmathe, made a strategic decision to transform the company into a world leader in nutrition, health, and wellness. Today, those original, less-healthy packaged foods make up less than half of Nestlé's product base, which tracks with the market shift toward healthier eating.[18]

Catalysts cause industries, markets, and geopolitical environments to shift. These shifts are happening more frequently. The normal course for a market-leading organization is to be significantly diminished when these shifts occur. Leaders must build structures with this in mind in order to be adaptable enough to survive and thrive amid these transitions.

Waiting for the transformation to manifest before considering your next move is not a productive strategy. There may not be enough time to act if we wait until the implications of the transformation to become obvious. Every industry will face its Amazon moment (or Uber, Apple, Netflix, Ford, and Bell moments). It is important for leaders to acknowledge this risk and ask themselves the extent to which they are willing to engage in the difficult exercise of change and transformation.

CHANGE MANAGEMENT WITHIN THE GOVERNMENT

Many government agencies feature similar dynamics as large corporations, but they also face unique challenges resulting from the nuances of operating in the public sector. In fact, change may even be a more arduous and protracted task in government than in the private sector, because governments can survive in mediocrity for far longer than businesses. The negative effects of not adapting to change, however, tend to be more wide-ranging in government than in the private sector, because failures to respond to changing conditions can correlate directly to health, education, defense, and quality-of-life issues for citizens.

In recent decades, not many federal policies have had as large a day-to-day impact on millions of Americans as the launch of the Affordable Care Act (ACA). The public face of this program was Healthcare.gov, the website portal through which users would access the system. Healthcare.gov was built via a government acquisition process that was designed before the internet and has not evolved with technology and the changing business environment. Shortly after passage of the ACA in 2010, the Department of Health and Human Services (DHHS) generated requirements, went through the competitive process, and awarded CGI Federal with a series of five contracts totaling $251 million to build, test, and maintain the exchange. The system quickly spiraled out of control when on October 1, 2013, millions of Americans logged on to Healthcare.gov hoping to shop for health insurance plans.

The website did not work, and the initial efforts to fix the system were indicative of the problem itself. Bloomberg's analysis of a DHHS inspector general report[19] demonstrates that there were ultimately sixty separate contracts totaling $799 million awarded by early 2014. In addition to CGI Federal's $251 million, Quality Software Services was awarded $164.9 million in contracts, as were HP Enterprise Services ($77.6 million), Terremark Federal Group ($48.9 million), Accenture ($45 million), IDL Solutions ($31.8 million), DEDE ($25.6 million), Lockheed Martin ($19.7 million), The Mitre Corporation ($17.4 million), Maricom Systems ($14.4 million), Quality Technology ($13.2 million), Booz Allen Hamilton ($12.5 million), and twenty-one other companies.

This is madness—and it is the direct result of applying a pre-digital revolution process to a fundamentally digital asset such as a website. The traditional US Government acquisition process involves writing down a specific list of every feature, user interface, bell, and whistle that the buyer wants in a product or service, then asking multiple vendors to submit bids to build it. At the core of this process is the idea that you can sit down and write out exactly what you are going to want—in many cases, before that object, website, or service exists.

This is fine for buying a bullet that needs to be of specific dimensions and quality so that it can be fired from a specific weapon system. We can argue whether it works for something more complex, such as a fighter aircraft. But this is simply not how software development works. Agile development, adaptive planning, and evolutionary design are the keys to successful software development in most cases and are often at odds with the requirements-based acquisition process.

To get the program back on track, President Obama directed his staff to set aside standard processes and recruited Jennifer Pahlka from Code for America, alongside a team of private sector engineers, to work around the clock to fix the site. This nontraditional plan to bring in a small team of private sector technology experts ultimately saved Healthcare.gov and the legislation's rollout. It also demonstrated how governments could utilize cutting-edge technology to deliver services that benefit citizens and their communities.

The size of government intensifies the challenges that private sector companies face when it comes to change management. Instead of shareholder meetings, government leaders must contend with the wishes of voters, who can be as—or even more—focused on near-term priorities as shareholders of public companies.

Some politicians and voters argue that government should be run like a business. In theory, this sounds reasonable. No business, after all, would openly tolerate some of the terrible bureaucratic inefficiencies often found in government. Nevertheless, government has certain limitations not found in businesses, which makes the comparison imprecise. A forceful business leader determined to pivot can unilaterally decide to stop providing a product or service. Government leaders, on the other hand, cannot remove a service without considering how it will impact the larger population and the commitments that have been made to citizens. Also, while businesses are designed around economic motivations, the role of government is to protect and enable the success of its citizenry. Sometimes it is difficult to see an immediate return on those types of investments.

A highly visible manifestation of this challenge is American infrastructure, which is in a near-catastrophic state of disrepair. In its most recent report, the American Society of Civil Engineers gave the country a mark of D+ in this area, cautioning that the infrastructure was at risk of failure. It estimates more than $4.5 trillion will be necessary to bring the grade up to a B.[20] The United States has not made major infrastructure decisions and investments in generations, still using infrastructure that was built in the 1950s and earlier. This has led to a generation of policy makers without the experience of building major infrastructure and a generation of voters without the experience of allowing major infrastructure to be built.

US INFRASTRUCTURE REPORT CARD
2017 ASSESSMENT FROM THE AMERICAN SOCIETY OF CIVIL ENGINEERS

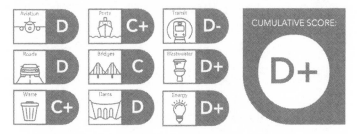

Source: "America's Grades," 2017 Infrastructure Report Card, https://www.infrastructurereportcard.org/americas-grades/.

Businesses do not provide legally mandated programs and services to people; businesses do not concern themselves with voters or election cycles. The challenge that government leaders face—to balance these pressures while planning for the future—is both difficult and crucial. When a business fails, shareholders lose money. When a government fails, the effects on people's lives are far more magnified and impactful.

THE UNIQUE CHALLENGES WITHIN ACADEMIA

Research and higher education institutions are extremely

important national assets that are equally impacted by technologies and socioeconomic forces that change the ways people live, work, and communicate. The purpose of academia, at its most basic definition, is to extend the pursuit of human knowledge and to prepare the next generation of citizens for great service in the workforce. Within academia, there is a debate on how to carry out this crucial dissemination of knowledge and how to best facilitate its pursuit.

Some advocate a narrow approach, believing the purpose of the educational institution is to only provide education to students. Other educators take a more expansive view of the educational system, thinking the mission compels them to engage with the broader community through research, advocating government policy, and partnering with industry.

This dispute has many obvious ramifications. It certainly influences the question of how academic institutions respond to major disruptions inside and outside the industry.

Leadership in academia is just as difficult as leadership in business and government in many respects. The same challenges and constraints exist for leaders within the higher education system, and they face similarly high pressure from the march of change. Consider, for example, the recent proliferation of nontraditional competitors in the academic sphere, such as YouTube lectures, Kahn Academy, or more structured MOOCs (massive open online courses), which in many cases are free. Penn State's recent acquisition of Kaplan, the online and print education juggernaut, is an interesting experiment to watch as universities work through the incorporation of different types of communication mediums into their educational models.

Paradigms change with lightning speed. For instance, technology changes at such a rapid pace that university degrees are no longer nearly as future-proof as they have been in the past; the expiration date on today's degrees gets shorter and shorter with each passing year and each new advancement. This puts enormous pressure on academia to rethink the way they educate and certify students in today's world.

Some universities, such as Stanford, have done better in partnering with companies, commercializing technology, and building startups based on the research done inside the university. Academics who stand to profit from their research will likely work harder toward product development and commercial applications, and collaboration with business helps academic institutions produce better-equipped graduates. Institutions such as Stanford and MIT prove that schools can benefit from a track record of successfully supported technology commercialization, not to mention the benefit that American businesses, governments, and consumers earn from this partnership.

The middle tier of the American university system—around five thousand institutions in the United States alone—is under a huge amount of pressure. With the advent of online degree options and an increasingly migratory population, people have more options and no longer necessarily go to college in the same region where they grow up. The result is that middle-tier regional schools are bleeding applicants and attendees at an accelerating rate. Many of these institutions are underwater, and are borrowing money to stay open. Leaders of these organizations have an extremely difficult challenge to adjust to these changes in order to ensure that their organizations remain relevant in this new world.

On a personal note, the alliance of academia and business is what made the multimodal aggregator app RideScout possible. When we began researching what it would take to organize all the world's modes of transportations, we soon discovered that universities from coast to coast had already identified the challenges required to build such a platform and had written about them in several white papers. The feedback from academia largely centered on the difficulties of the technology, although nobody had the appetite or incentive to take risks beyond their research to try to come up with the system that would overcome the barriers they were describing. Many in academia saw the opportunity of a seamless world of connectivity, but they could not—or chose not to—create the capacity to move it forward into the world. This experience is representative of the reasons why academia, government, and the private sector must find a better way to coexist.

THE CASUALTIES OF SUCCESS

Roughly twenty years ago, Clayton Christensen coined the term *disruptive innovation* to describe the phenomenon around how innovation disrupts industries.[21] His seminal book, *The Innovator's Dilemma*, describes the predicament leaders face when innovation competes with a company's core products. The root of his argument is that new products—almost by definition—take market share from the old products that they replace. Cannibalizing an existing product line threatens a company's profitability, which is why companies struggle to fully embrace innovation. In our experience, the dynamic that Christensen described is exacerbated by the human dimension, as leaders tend to focus their capital and best people on current product lines instead of developing ways to effectively disrupt themselves.

An emphasis on winning in the *now* often leads the major structures of a company to effectively inhibit innovation.

We argue that the concept of the innovator's dilemma happens subconsciously at the level of resource allocation within a company. There are essentially no leaders who deliberately decide or make company policy to not innovate. Instead, resources, talent, and incentives flow toward the divisions that make the company money. If one division generates the majority of the profits, then it will also receive the majority of the bonuses and career enhancement incentives. This department is not going to be the R&D department, which is a cost center as opposed to a profit center. As a result, R&D and innovation centers can become a difficult, less financially rewarding, and potentially risky place in the company to work, as that is where cuts are often made in times of financial stress. Talent and resources gravitate to where the action and reward happens, which leads to underfunded and ineffective corporate R&D arms.

It is not that companies are building the next big thing and failing to monetize it, as Christensen depicted using the example of disk drives in the 1980s and 1990s—they are not building the next big thing, period. Their best people are sucked into the machine of the *now*. Innovation is underresourced and underfunded.

Essentially, leaders rarely even get to the innovator's dilemma. They hardly ever make it to the point where they have to make a deliberate decision about whether to risk cannibalizing the current business with a great new product, because, more often than not, the R&D department never developed the great new product in the first place. In many cases, it was a startup in California or Texas that ultimately developed that next great product instead.

The challenges to innovation in the public sector are different, but in many cases, they are also derived from a structurally driven adherence to the status quo, just as the challenges the other sectors face. One of the many ways this is manifested is in the problem of distributed costs and concentrated benefits. These situations occur when the costs of a program or government investment are borne broadly via taxation or other means, but the benefit of that program is localized in a community or company. The people who bear the costs pay only a little per individual, so they often do not care enough to exert time and resources challenging the validity of the program. The people who receive the benefit care deeply and invest heavily in the program to ensure its endurance.

Our entire society could suffer long-term stagnation and miss out on the benefits of innovation, simply because the distributed costs and entrenched stakeholders prevent us from revising or replacing outdated systems with tools, processes, and resources that are better applied to the problems of tomorrow as opposed to the questions of yesterday.

People, in general, tend to avoid risk and gravitate toward the comfort and predictability of the status quo. When it comes down to it, organizations are nothing more than collections of people. As Peter Drucker is attributed to have said, "Culture eats strategy for breakfast." Creating an organization with a nimble, inclusive, and innovative culture can make all the difference when it comes to innovating, but these cultures need to be built with an understanding of human behavioral drivers, and they need to be supported by financial structures that align incentives with desired behavior. A win-now environment, for example, where compensation reflects maximizing profits and minimizing costs, will result in a certain type of behavior that may or may not be aligned with the long-term goals of the organization.

It is easy for some to view government as a faceless big brother and academics as aloof elitists who ruminate in their ivory towers. Likewise, we often think of companies through the narrow lens of the products they produce. If a company is producing cool, trendy products, it must be a forward-looking company. In reality, all organizations, including government and academia, are defined more by the people than the products put out into the world; and these people, for better or worse, often have priorities that run counter to the organization unless they are deliberately aligned.

Employment, after all, for many people, is simply a way

to support personal, familial, spiritual, and political priorities. People have different reasons to be motivated toward a variety of outcomes. Workers are also mobile and have options; at any time, most workers can decide to pursue their careers at other companies. Their fates are not inexorably tied to the organization. There are many examples of people demonstrating personal success amid a larger organizational failure. It is not uncommon to find an employee or even a leader acting in a fashion that runs against the organization's current strategy. It takes deliberate effort to bring together individual and organizational priorities, as they both change over time.

Companies, academic institutions, and government institutions are groups of individuals with a complex symphony of motives, desires, hopes, and dreams. Ignoring the internal elements or culture of the company while trying to manage change is as dangerous for a leader as disregarding market shifts. If leaders plan to shift an organization's focus, they must pay attention to workforce concerns such as incentives, compensation, pride, motivation, and alignment—all in addition to the organization's overall strategy.

Leadership in the face of changing environmental conditions is a complex balancing act, and we do not necessarily have the luxury of picking and choosing the problem sets we seek to deal with. Opposition and roadblocks will appear in different and unexpected areas, and the microperspective of personal dynamics must always be considered within or in balance with the macroperspective of organizational priorities. The human element makes change management difficult, but there are concrete steps we can take to prevent these potential obstacles from holding us back as we shift to meet the demands of a changing world.

Leading your organization through a strategic shift requires a fundamental understanding of human nature. Most of us perceive the world through a lens of values and beliefs instilled in us from the time of our childhood. Major changes in an organization will face institutional resistance because individuals tend to start from a position of resistance when they encounter something new. These people have been working a certain way for years, and they will likely remain out of step with new processes unless they are intentionally brought into the fold.

Compassionate, proactive leadership is the key element in any shift. We are well past the hierarchal era that believes the leader can drive organizational success all on his or her own, but there must be a compass that directs the working parts toward the overarching strategy. This is the person or group in the organization who sees something significant about the evolving environment that is not readily apparent to the larger body, the person who can see both opportunity and threat. Once the environment is understood and that vision is established, the psychological and financial incentives can then be aligned to facilitate change.

BUILDING ADAPTABLE ORGANIZATIONS

Adaptable organizations, that thrive in times of transformation, excel at aligning strategy, culture, and behavioral incentives. Alignment makes them proactive, risk-tolerant, and focused on a shared vision for the future. While change in organizations is naturally inhibited by psychological and institutional biases towards the status quo, resources exist to help leaders reorient teams and facilitate organizational agility and flexibility.

Change is coming. There is no way to avoid it. Our task is to build adaptable organizations that can thrive in times of transformation.

It is crucial to understand and fully embody this to effectively guide an organization in the years to come. Institutions and organizational principles that are designed for optimization and efficiency are different than those designed for agility and strategic flexibility. Most industry-leading organizations are designed for efficiency and as such will be extremely stressed during periods of change. This is not indicative of poor leadership or ineffective teams; it is simply the nature of how most organizations have evolved. However, it is possible to position for agility, even while maintaining efficient operations.

When we break this process down, there are three essential tasks that organizations need to be able to execute to adjust to major change.

1. Identify that a significant shift is occurring that will impact the organization with enough time to react. This is a function of intelligence.
2. Decide whether and how to react. This is a function of strategy.
3. Align the organization to the new strategy. This is a function of leadership, change management, and organizational design.

While this seems simple, and is in concept, let us remember that most companies do not do this successfully. Even the really good organizations that have grown to positions of industry leadership rarely manage to adapt successfully to a transition forced on them by a significant market shift. There are many structural land mines in the way of leading an organization through change, and successful execution of these three steps requires flexibility, agility, and decisiveness.

INNOVATION MODELS

Innovation is the starting point for flexibility and agility, as it provides both insight into emerging change and tools to adapt. The best way for public and private sector leaders to proactively identify important emerging technological catalysts is to connect their organizations to the global innovation ecosystem, either directly or indirectly. Prior to the 1960s, the most common way for an organization to innovate was through R&D labs inside the company. Company leadership would direct engineers to work on particular priorities. The company would test an invention's commercial viability, and if all went well, they would adopt it as a product or service.

This model of innovation works in many cases and has produced many of the great innovations we use today, but is structurally difficult to implement in large, efficient organizations because of problems discussed earlier, such as human and financial capital allocation challenges. As venture capital and private equity matured into a robust financial intermediary role over the past twenty-five to thirty-five years, other approaches to corporate innovation have emerged.

The internal innovation model still persists, but on the other end of the spectrum, we find an external innovation model that uses capital markets to absorb the developmental and organizational risk associated with innovation.

In the external innovation model, companies make the deliberate decision to innovate via mergers and acquisitions, working with startups and venture capitalists who are developing and funding new technologies. In this approach, a company sits back and watches the dozens or hundreds of different startups pursue the desired technology. When a startup figures it out and the technology reaches the point of maturity, the company buys the startup and makes it a product or business unit to build on.

In many cases, companies often are forced to pay a multiple above what internal development would have cost, but this approach serves to outsource many of the risks of innovation—but not integration—to entrepreneurs and investors that operate in this ecosystem. The company does not have to fund technology approaches they do not know are going to work, and they do not have to manage the organizational challenge of being both an efficient mature-market company and an innovative new-market company at the same time, which as we have noted, is extremely difficult.

CORPORATE INNOVATION MODELS
TYPES OF INNOVATION PROGRAMS BASED ON CULTURE, RESOURCES, AND OBJECTIVES

INTERNAL INNOVATION	TRADITIONAL R&D	OFFSITE INNOVATION CENTERS	INTERNAL DISRUPTION TEAMS
BLENDED MODEL	CORPORATE VENTURE CAPITAL	HOSTED INCUBATORS & ACCELERATORS	JOINT VENTURE R&D
EXTERNAL INNOVATION	MERGERS AND ACQUISITIONS	3RD PARTY VENTURE CAPITAL INVESTMENTS	OUTSOURCED TECHNOLOGY SCOUTING

In between those two opposite ends of the spectrum—internal and external innovation—there are blended innovation models that take on a variety of different shapes and forms based on industry dynamics and company culture. Some companies manage internal investment groups, similar to venture capital funds. Corporate venture capital is similar in some aspects to the external innovation model, but it tends to invest noncontrolling positions in companies that have not yet "won" a market or product category and still require significant joint development post acquisition.

Others host internal incubators, where they not only own part of the startups, but they also encourage other entrepreneurs to participate in order to see what innovations are happening in their industry or focus area. There are many examples of these types of programs across a variety of industries: Daimler's Mobility X Lab, IBM Alpha Zone Accelerator, Wells Fargo Startup Accelerator, Sprint Accelerator, Citi Ventures Accelerator, Budweiser Dream Brewery, Cisco Entrepreneurs in Residence, and the Bridge by Coca-Cola are prominent examples, but there are hundreds of these types of programs.[22] In some instances, companies will invest as limited partners in third-party venture capital funds to leverage professional investors to scout technologies more broadly, either as a complement to or substitute for an internal corporate venture capital team.

This is not a one-size-fits-all approach. Different models are right for different types of companies. Your organization's corporate culture, objectives, team, financial position, and strategic relationships are all key determinants toward the right model. The time horizon is also extremely important, as many innovation efforts take years or decades in order to be productive. As a reference point, most venture capital funds are designed for ten-year life cycles, and successful venture capitalists operate multiple funds simultaneously. Long-term investments need to be managed accordingly, which is another challenge for many publicly traded companies that are driven by short-term pressures.

Commitment and consistency are important elements to any type of corporate innovation and long-term planning, and it is crucial to secure organizational commitment before attempting any long-term activity. Despite the inevitable leadership transitions, enduring organizations must have the staying power to execute long-term strategy. This is an element that companies often claim but less often live up to, especially when the environment becomes difficult and leaders are pushed to "do something." Balancing the pressures to change strategy, the disruption associated with changing strategy, and the need to change when you realize that your strategy is not going to work is a central leadership challenge of the modern era.

Government organizations also use different innovation models that are evolving alongside the private sector. In-Q-Tel, for example, is effectively a venture capital fund run on behalf of the Central Intelligence Agency and broader US intelligence community.[23] The Department of Defense has a variety of different mechanisms through which it develops technologies, ranging from in-house innovation teams at the Defense Innovation Unit Experimental (DIUx), or development through the Defense Advanced Research Projects Agency (DARPA), to partnerships such as Cooperative Research and Development Agreements (CRADA), and outsourced models using competed Research, Development, Test, and Evaluation (RDT&E) contracts. Just as with the private sector, there is no one-size-fits-all approach in the public sector.

RISK MANAGEMENT FRAMEWORKS

Participating in the innovation ecosystem allows us to view some subset of the development that may ultimately impact our organizations. However, it is impossible to focus everywhere. A useful tool to help identify the fields and types of developments that could have a significant impact is a formal risk management system. Risk management processes and systems allow us to see vulnerabilities and points of exposure or leverage so that we can focus resources to mitigate risks or pursue opportunities for growth in these areas.

Our advocacy of these tools is a result of having grown up with these systems in the military. We have witnessed firsthand how a risk management approach can be a useful tool in helping focus an organization on the technologies, risks, or events that have the potential to truly disrupt the strategic landscape. It allows leaders to place resources and personal focus at the center of gravity, where the organization is most exposed.

The US Army uses a risk management framework that requires its leaders to think about risks in terms of both likelihood of occurrence and severity of impact, which we believe can be illustrative for business and public sector leaders. When a unit goes out for training, for example, there is a risk that a soldier will suffer from dehydration. Mild dehydration represents a medium-high probability risk that carries a low impact if basic mediation elements are in place such as water, shade, awareness, and so forth. Conversely, a soldier getting wounded by overhead fires from a helicopter during a training exercise is a low-probability risk with an extremely severe impact. Regardless of the probability of occurrence, the potential severity means that risk must be mitigated, even if the effort consumes a disproportionate amount of the organization's resources.

This framework forces us to focus on high-impact, existential issues in opposition to the natural tendency to dismiss those risks simply because they are not likely to happen. In this example, protection from catastrophic downside risk is more important than 100 percent efficiency. Businesses would benefit from this approach, even though it does not necessarily align with an optimal use of resources.

Understand that history is littered with organizations that failed to believe a significant risk or risks could possibly happen. Because they dismissed those risks as unlikely, they did not monitor or take steps to mitigate them. A simple question could be illustrative: what are the catastrophic events that our organization simply cannot allow to happen, and how are we aligned toward identifying and preventing those risks from occurring? These could be new technologies, policy decisions, competitor behavior, changing customer dynamics, or any number of factors.

There are a number of different approaches that organizations can take to understand and mitigate risk. A common approach that we see across industries is to invest in new technology as a hedging strategy, which provides both an intimate understanding of what is happening in the field and allows the company to benefit from the shift if it were to happen. This may manifest as R&D in the anticipated technologies, or mergers and acquisitions activity with companies involved in the area of risk or opportunity.

A risk management framework helps to identify where to focus your energy, talent, and capital to reduce risk or participate in the opportunity that change brings. In some cases, this can mean developing mitigation or hedging strategies; in other cases, it can drive leaders to buy companies, stand up new divisions, or invest in specific types of "moonshot" R&D activities.

Daimler took this framework to its Mercedes-Benz shareholders when the CEO told them they were moving away from being a manufacturing company to become a mobility services provider. This came after evaluation of the risks of autonomous vehicles and mobility-as-a-service providers such as Uber and Lyft. In an attempt to ensure its position of market leadership, the company is now working on autonomous vehicle technology, electric drivetrain technology, mobility payment systems and apps, and other technologies and business models to mitigate the risk of being left behind or displaced as the transportation industry radically shifts in upcoming years.

Ultimately, risk management is about prioritization and focus. Just like we prioritize within our day-to-day tasks, we must prioritize within the hierarchy of business, strategy, and operational risk. Without a framework in place, every task tends to become a priority of equal importance. Structure provides perspective so that you can evaluate the tasks at hand and focus on the ones that are truly most important.

Even though we call this a risk management framework, it can also be useful for identifying transformational opportunities. Similar to risks, we can identify what changes would create the biggest positive opportunities and focus resources to make them reality.

The risk management framework provides a simple approach to decide how to focus an organization's efforts. The application of this framework is different for each company and organization, but it remains an important tool to help separate the signal from the noise and work on things that are really important—as opposed to things that simply *seem* important or things that need to be done *now*. It is impossible to focus everywhere at once, and an organization—and a leader, for that matter—has only so much bandwidth for strategic initiatives. Knowing this limitation, it is crucial to focus on the areas that will have the largest and most necessary organization-wide impact.

Culture is the perfect place to start.

CREATING A CULTURE OF FLEXIBILITY AND AGILITY

When large organizations consider strategy in response to market shifts, it is important to note that, most often, the costs of inaction are far greater than the cost of an incorrect—or a marginally correct—action. Even if the incorrect or unsuccessful action costs billions, these activities are appropriate when done to mitigate far greater potential risks. As such, we suggest a bias toward action. Action creates insights and options, and facilitates a proactive posture that is far easier to adjust from than a reactive posture and culture.

There is no such thing as perfect information in complex endeavors, such as transformation in the face of unknown future risk. Leaders are paid to use judgment and make decisions with incomplete information while accepting responsibility for the eventual outcome. The speed of market changes is too fast, and it is impossible to have clarity regarding what is coming next unless you wait until change happens, at which point it is often too late to effectively respond. Action, even in a way that turns out to be only marginally correct, provides a first step from which you can course-correct as the environment continues to change.

As a society, we tend to think of CEOs and elected officials as the change agents and unilateral decision makers in organizations. In reality, these men and women have their focus spread extremely thin and are more constrained by the organization and the environment than most external observers appreciate. As we are in a world where most of these new developments result from cutting-edge technological research, many drivers of change will emerge from fields where the senior leader in an organization does not have the specific expertise to fully understand what is happening. Senior leaders, by nature, cannot be experts in everything, which creates a challenge when expertise is required to understand emerging change.

This expands the issue past the capacity of the CEO or elected official, as leaders at every level of the organization need to keep their focus on the second and third order significance of emerging developments. If they think something important is emerging, they must have the courage to speak, and the organization must have the structures in place to listen. With firsthand, tactical knowledge of the business, frontline leaders must be respected and empowered to support technology identification and strategy transformation. Effective senior leadership is not achieved by CEOs being expert in everything; it is achieved by creating channels and processes that allow these insights to be brought to light.

Another common mistake is when leaders think the heavy lifting is about coming up with the strategy, as opposed to the process of communication and alignment that makes teams comfortable and willing proponents of the strategic shift. We find an example of this challenge in the transportation business.

A decade ago, one of the nation's largest taxi providers was sitting on a comfortable monopoly. The leaders clearly saw how mobile and location-based technology would disrupt the industry, so they created an app for riders to find taxis with more ease. The app never took off because drivers never used it, and fundamentally disruptive rideshare companies such as Uber and Lyft came along and succeeded where the taxi industry had failed to evolve. Despite seeing the change coming, the taxi industry did not embrace the rideshare phenomenon, because at the frontline-leader level, they did not believe they had to change. The senior leadership, who had been in the business for decades, could not shift the internal culture, such as convincing drivers and shareholders to accept different pricing models and costs of entry for drivers. They faced a combination of different factors that inhibited change—they did not see themselves as having any competition, incentives were not aligned toward change, the need and benefit for change was not effectively communicated, and organizational structures were not up to the task of directing behavioral change.

The alignment of strategy, incentives, and organizational structures is extremely important. In most city taxi companies, the owners of the companies are rarely doing the actual driving. Rather, taxi drivers are independent contractors required to own their own car or finance it from the cab company owners. Usually, the drivers lease or license the taxi medallion. The drivers rent the taxi dispatch machine, the payment processing machine, and all communication devices. Income is derived from the fees paid by the drivers into the cab company. The result of this arrangement is that cab company owners did not personally experience a drop in revenue due to the popularity of Uber and Lyft—only their drivers struggled to turn a profit. There is very little incentive for the cab companies to modernize; their customers are the *drivers*, not the passengers, and the drivers will have to pay fees to the cab company regardless of whether the end-user experience is good or bad. The drivers, concordantly, feel the pain of the industry disruption but are not positioned to change and innovate within the cab company—they do not make the rules.

In addition, these organizations underappreciated the

likelihood of risk. Cab company owners firmly believed that in the end, companies such as Uber and Lyft were illegal and would never be allowed to compete. In other words, the company's leaders thought of it as a *legal* issue instead of a problem of innovation. This is surprisingly common, and it is important to note that despite the best efforts of many to the contrary, litigation is not a viable transformation or innovation strategy. Location-based mobile technology has enabled a market shift that is not going to go away, and taxi companies will not recover the ground they have lost.

Creating a culture of flexibility and agility requires incentives that reward—or at minimum do not punish—people who ask why and act to make the organization better, even when they step outside the bounds of their job descriptions. To survive in the current landscape, organizational structures need to be built around agility, creativity, and adaptability—even though this will sometimes require a slight tradeoff in efficiency and operating margins.

Public institutions suffer from identical challenges related to an organizational design created during the industrial era. The term *red tape* comes from the period following the Civil War, when the Veterans Administration would collect all of a veteran's files in large binders kept together by red tape. To cut through the red tape meant to get access to one's personnel files, which was an arduous and lengthy process. It is no secret that bureaucracy resulting from processes once designed for efficiency tends to slow down government. Voters despise red tape and will not accept failure, just as shareholders react to companies missing quarterly financial targets. This creates an environment in which public sector leaders, especially politicians, tend to be extremely risk-averse. They will usually shy away from innovative pilot programs and change in general, even when they realize that it is necessary. Innovators and intrapreneurs who can overcome these challenges are needed at all levels of the public sector, just as they are in the private sector.

Developing a culture of innovation and agility within an organization requires focus and investment, and a willingness to support activities that are future-oriented. Do your employees attend conferences or knowledge exchange events, even when they only tangentially relate to the organization's mission? Does the system allow for travel and continuing education? Do you have book clubs and leadership development programs within the organization to encourage group thinking about a variety of subjects? Is time reserved at the end of the workweek to discuss ideas outside the normal day-to-day operations?

These programs decentralize the organization and empower individuals to learn new things, which will lead them to try different things and look at problems in different ways. Institutionalizing the ideas of innovators within an organization via a feedback system where you can learn from these internal pioneers what is working and what is not is a key component of agile cultures and is necessary for all three stages of the transformation process.

CORPORATE NEAR-DEATH EXPERIENCES

Many of the companies that have succeeded in reinventing themselves did so in response to the business equivalent of life-or-death pressures. In many of these cases, the real possibility of losing everything allowed them to align everyone inside the organization with the need for transformation.

In the 1990s, the top competitor for US car manufacturers was Japan, and the way to get ahead in that competition was through the faster development of new models. The stark need for a speedier design and development process led US companies to turn to computational structural dynamics, or CSD, a branch of structural mechanics that uses numerical analysis and data structures to solve and analyze structural problems. By reducing the volume of crash testing needed for each new model, the turn to CSD drastically lowered development time for a new car from seven to three years.[24]

American companies were forced to innovate in response

to the existential threat of foreign competition. These changes were painful and resulted in new workflows, business processes, and organizational structures. Some groups within these organizations became more important and others became less important throughout this transition. Regardless of the understandable discomfort that results from having to learn how to work differently, US automobile manufacturers were able to manage change because everyone in these organizations understood that if they did not change, the company could fail and they may no longer have jobs. The sharp understanding of the risk of losing everything allowed these organizations to overcome the internal barriers to change.

Similarly, and around the same time period, US oil and gas companies faced a much lower success rate than today on new holes drilled; each dry hole that did not contain oil could cost a loss of up to $100 million or more. This led companies to adopt a technology called computational seismic depth migration to provide a new way of understanding geology that increased their hit rate significantly.[25] Geologists, although initially reticent, were forced to evolve their processes as the costs of drilling increased, and companies were no longer able to withstand the levels of inaccuracy that had previously been the norm.

There are clear lessons that we can extract from these

and other corporate near-death experiences in order to infuse them in our organizations. For leaders, the obvious motivation is to not have to wait for life-or-death pressure to occur in order to achieve the organizational alignment needed to change; most companies, in fact, do not make it out of these situations alive. Still, we can benefit from studying organizations that survived near-death experiences to identify elements that enabled these companies to transform.

There are several commonalities that we see in the corporate near-death situations. First is that the imperative for swift decision making at the highest levels of company leadership acts as a forcing function in these situations; leaders are left with no alternative but to act. Second is that clear and effective communications in the surviving companies was paramount. Leaders in those organizations shared the situation, mission, and plan in such a fashion that everyone understood exactly what was at stake. Third is that organizational alignment to the transformation strategy established in the surviving organizations was key. These teams wholly bought in to the necessity of transformation, which helped to break down institutional barriers to change.

All three of these commonalities are features that leaders can build toward, even when they are not facing life-or-death pressures. While it may have been easier for leaders of organizations that were experiencing life-or-death pressures to be decisive because they did not have the luxury to "wait and see" and move with the herd, decisiveness does not require external pressure. Rather, it requires accurate information and courage on behalf of leaders. Organizations that effectively transform act clearly and decisively.

Effective leaders communicate their decisions widely. Everyone in the organization needs to know how important their work is, how real the threats are, and how those threats connect to their careers. The form this takes could be as simple as sending out newsletters, holding leader discussion forums, or sharing key performance indicators and company metrics broadly, as opposed to holding them close within the executive team. We do not need to wait until an existential threat emerges to communicate clearly to our organizations around strategy and emerging threats and opportunities.

The most difficult of these challenges is the issue of organizational alignment and breaking old processes in favor of new, which is unquestionably facilitated by a well-understood threat. However, it is possible for leaders to work toward organizational alignment without being motivated by a dire threat; we can align organization charts, incentives, and personal motivators toward change in order to get everyone moving in the same direction.

This may happen more slowly without a clear external motivator, but it can be done, and misalignment of strategy and incentives is a common error that must be avoided.

All of these factors build toward the requirement for a culture of innovation and flexibility. Proactive leaders enable each other and attract other talent who want to work at a company where they know that they can make a difference if they have the idea, even if they are not a senior executive by role. The most talented people we have worked with put themselves in environments where they can be heard and where they know they can contribute.

DISMANTLING ORGANIZATIONAL SILOS

The drive toward efficiency and economies of scale in the past one hundred years has resulted in specialization and bureaucracy, which tend to ossify organizations and inspire priorities that may diverge from those of the company as a whole. Subcultures are natural within large organizations, and activities that foster cohesion and even some types of competition can be productive when placed in context of overall organizational strategy. The challenge lies in preventing silos from growing so ossified that they act out of sync with the organization's priorities, like companies within companies. This is never intentional but is so prevalent across industries and government institutions that it merits focus.

Take sales, for example. We may notice that the salespeople talk on phones a lot, which can be distracting to engineers, so we separate them from the quieter work areas. Thus begins the creation of an unintentional silo, which forms the basis of that team's subculture. Perhaps isolation from the rest of the company becomes a matter of pride and identity for the group. The salespeople, who essentially work in an echo chamber that reinforces their priorities and assumptions, cannot understand why the technology department is not providing what they need, when they need it. It becomes easier to speculate about other groups than to work directly with them to understand key issues. The sales team might then hire a technology specialist to implement the technology department's directives, rather than walk down the hall to interact with the tech department and bridge the gap themselves. Meanwhile, the product development side decides the salespeople would be superfluous if only the engineers could be left alone to develop a product that can sell itself. In this way, rivalries develop to the point that each silo or department functions independently rather than as parts of a working whole.

Regardless of how well-intentioned these actions began, at the end of the day they result in two or more groups who think very differently about the business and its core issues. Now, on top of this ecosystem, layer questions about why sales or product performance have not been as good as everyone had hoped, with very real implications for the careers and paychecks of those involved. We then create an incentive to define challenges in terms of external drivers—sales blames engineering and vice versa. We have thus created two different silos with sometimes converging and other times diverging interests that may or may not be aligned with the overall goals of the organization.

Most companies undergo a natural process wherein teams settle into silos that serve to divide the organization. Within each of these silos, great ideas about innovation and the future emerge, but they cannot connect with the receptive minds in other parts of the organization. Too much of the rest of the organization is blocked off by location, precedent, or culture. Because many of the issues that we face today are multidisciplinary and complex by nature, organizational silos can severely inhibit change and growth.

Silos also pose a major roadblock when a leader identifies a market shift and develops a response. When it is time to align the organization with that strategy, competing interests among the silos severely diminish the organization's ability to implement strategy. Each silo will be concerned about how the changes will impact their group. Obviously, efficient business processes are a positive element of cohesive teams, but when efficiency results in bureaucracy or silos that develop their own priorities in conflict with the overall organizational priorities, those silos become a serious problem and an impassible obstacle to change.

How can companies best dismantle silos and unify their processes and priorities across the entire organization?

The first and most critical element is the realignment of individual incentives with the goals of the organization, not just within a particular silo. This can be done a number of different ways, but a thoughtful organizational approach that connects compensation, equity awards, commissions, and performance review criteria to organizational goals is essential. Incentivizing cross-team knowledge sharing, communicating, and even direct collaboration with clear and actionable rewards is key to motivating teams to unify with the organization's larger goals.

A second important way to break down silos is cross-training. Sales has a much better picture of the needs of the development team, and vice versa, if each team is cross-trained in the others' unique requirements and challenges. This process of seeing firsthand that our coworkers have difficult jobs and are working hard enables mutual respect, trust, and cohesion. Even if cross-training happens at the short-term expense of productivity, the long-term benefit exceeds that cost in comparison as teams begin to form priorities based on not just their own needs but the needs of the company as a whole.

The more we can disrupt a person's perspective and provide a broader experience, the more clearly they will be able to see the overall vision of why change is necessary and how it can be implemented. Facilitating incidental contact between silos should be a focus at every level of the company. Top leadership and mid-level managers of different departments and areas must create the space to come together and exchange ideas.

In the military, officers must have joint assignments, working directly and collaboratively with their peers in other services in order to be promoted to senior ranks. (This was not easy, by the way—Congress had to use law to force the services to work together in the Goldwater-Nichols Department of Defense Reorganization Act of 1986.) Professors take sabbaticals and teach at other universities. An interesting example is that the produce we enjoy today tastes, looks, and survives better because we have combined variants of different species in order to make the end result better. When the silos of our organization begin to break down and individuals take the time to walk in their coworkers' shoes, they become more willing and in some cases eager to work together. Salespeople remember that the developers do not get feedback from clients, so they start passing information along. Developers understand more of what the salespeople face when trying to sell, so they seek advice when designing future products.

The organizations we admire are those that have responded to rapid change by unchaining and enabling their people, giving them tools to obtain a broader perspective and freedom to make decisions that affect the organization. Where we have people sit and how we facilitate interaction between different parts of the organization seems mundane but in reality affects our ability to grow and adapt as conditions change.

ALIGNMENT OF INCENTIVES

Incentives do not merely take on the shape of money. Compensation is important, but incentives are often even more effective when they offer boosts in status and career trajectory: promotions, career development, and other nonfinancial benefits.

Just as we need to understand the basics of behavioral psychology in order to identify roadblocks toward implementing organizational change, it can also help us design systems of incentives to align behavior with long-term organizational objectives. In times of change, nonfinancial incentives can be tied to clarity around performance metrics and promotion milestones, to give team members confidence that even though organizational dynamics are changing, they will still have a role. Some organizations try to make work more enjoyable via team activities, flexible schedules, and perks—which helps anchor commitment to the organization. Other areas of focus are public award and commendation systems to elevate team members who proactively support organizational strategies.

An often-overlooked incentive to motivate desired behavior is to remove team members who underperform or are negative toward the organization's desired transformation from the organization entirely. In some cases, the most effective way to reward good performance is to punish poor performance, which serves to both remove roadblocks and to signal to those who are doing what they are supposed to that they have chosen the right path and that the organization is serious about transformation.

Organizations must discover for themselves the most natural and effective ways to incentivize behavior in support of their goals. We also need to be wary of unintended consequences when adjusting incentive programs. In the 1990s, politicians decided communities were stronger when families worked to provide for themselves, which meant that people would be expected to prove they were working if they were to receive welfare money. As a result, single moms in particular were left spending more time working and less time with their children, which had the second order effect of creating a breakdown in community which we still wrestle with today. If our goals are to create better communities that raise stronger kids, we should be extremely wary of policies that detract from parenting.

Transforming a large organization successfully requires use of every advantage you can find. In many cases, this means it can be important to complement your industry expertise with best practices from both the private and public sectors. It might make sense to hire teams dedicated to researching change that is occurring in other industries; in other situations, that expertise is better brought in as needed. In other cases, it will be more efficient to use partners who can provide insights about the specific developments that are emerging outside your core industry. Sometimes, we benefit from an independent perspective to help connect the dots—even those dots that seem to have little connection to your current operations.

We created the Grayline Group in response to the need for cross-industry expertise to help organizations make decisions in the face of emerging cross-industry shifts. So many variables are changing simultaneously, and it can be cost prohibitive for organizations to try and cover all the fields where change is happening. Most leaders understand that it is inefficient, and in many cases impossible, to be an expert in everything, which is true regardless of the size of an organization. This leads us to the next section—an overview of the catalyst framework, which will be followed by a specific discussion of some of the emerging global transformations that we believe will impact all public and private sector organizations.

PART TWO

CATALYSTS

WHAT ARE CATALYSTS?

It is crucial to identify the inflection points that lead to transformations and paradigm shifts in markets before they happen. While it is difficult to separate the signal from the noise in the modern environment of information overload and media hysteria, it is possible to build a methodology and decision-making framework to evaluate emerging developments in the context of their potential for system-wide, transformational effects.

This is a fascinating time to be alive. Within the next decade, we anticipate several significant shifts that will fundamentally impact global markets. Transformations of this magnitude, which affect every industry and region, used to happen once in a generation. There has never been a time with so much change, so quickly. Manufacturing is on the brink of a revolution, thanks to 3D printing technology; in the energy sector, renewables are becoming economically viable as a result of advancements in energy storage technology; machine learning, augmented reality, and genomic technologies are reaching maturity. Cities are growing larger than ever before and incorporating new types of technology-enabled infrastructure. The changing demographic profile of the first world will significantly impact markets and social institutions.

It is important to begin this discussion by pointing out that society is resilient. In the past, during periods of accelerated change, our social, political, and economic institutions have adapted. While these transitions can be painful on the micro scale—at the level of a company or public institution, for example—on the macro, global scale, the larger ecosystems in which our organizations operate are resilient. While we are optimistic about the future in a macro sense, most of our discussion is focused on the disruptive nature of these catalysts in order to help leaders understand and prepare.

Markets, technologies, and social systems tend not to advance in a linear fashion. Trace back the history of any market development and you will notice a step function built around the specific inflection points that introduce a new paradigm for the operation of that system. In essence, systems incrementally progress until something significant happens that changes the fundamentals of the system and establishes a new normal. At that point, incremental improvements continue for a period until, suddenly, there is another giant step up to the next plateau. The time between these inflection points varies in different industries and geographies, ranging from centuries to decades or less. We see this pattern most clearly in technology developments, although the same model can be applied to political and social systems.

These inflection points are what we call catalysts. Catalysts are the truly transformational shifts that emerge from the culmination of decades of smaller incremental developments. Catalysts represent a paradigm shift or step function change in markets and/or political, economic, and social systems, changing the fundamental conditions on which all organizations develop strategy. The telegraph was a catalyst. A more reliable telegraph was an incremental improvement. The personal computer was a catalyst. Faster computers that enabled more efficient processing were incremental improvements. Commercial aviation was a catalyst. Cheaper and safer flight options are incremental improvements.

Identifying emerging catalysts is among the most important efforts that organizations can undertake. Many organizations excel in the periods between market shifts, during an environment of incremental growth. Most companies are built for efficiency and excellence amid gradual environmental changes. Very few organizations, however, are built for periods of transformation, which, as we have discussed, are coming more rapidly. It is extremely difficult to identify a catalyst before it happens, correctly understand the impact it will have on one's operation, and successfully transform to seize the opportunities created by the new paradigm.

Our risk management framework is designed to help organizations identify the areas where they are most exposed to facilitate focus on the fields where change will result in the most significant impact. Identifying these changes that are transformational is a challenge in the current media environment. We are drowning in noise. Many developments are positioned to be paradigm-altering when, in reality, they are incremental improvements of limited systemic importance. The current business model of media (entertainment) drives media companies to position everything as spectacular and momentous, which exacerbates the challenge of sorting the signal from the noise. Our inboxes, televisions, and web browsers are flooded by bold proclamations on a variety of topics, and it is all too easy to believe what we are repeatedly told— the country is falling apart, a new widget will change the world, and so on. Leaders must absorb huge volumes of information with discernment and accuracy.

Another challenge is that technology is increasingly complicated and specialized, so that a nonexpert cannot easily examine developments in another field with any degree of confidence. In an environment where the pace of change is accelerating, we are confronted with many important developments. Although few will turn out to be transformational, they must all be understood, which does not come easily for the nonexpert and we are all nonexperts in topics outside of our core areas of focus.

In response to these challenges, we have developed a framework and methodology to help identify catalysts—the inflection points of transformation that we see as being broadly and structurally important to the global system. This is not a one-size-fits-all approach. Different types of evaluation systems will be needed for different types of companies and public institutions, but our view is that a systematic data-driven approach is required to see these transformations in the windshield as opposed to the rearview mirror. New winners and losers emerge as markets shift in response to these inflection points. Identifying both the opportunity and risk amid these transformations is crucial as market and geopolitical hierarchies are reordered during these periods in favor of those who are able to capitalize on change.

HOW TO SPOT A CATALYST

Maslow's hierarchy of needs builds basic human requirements and desires upon one another, with physiological needs forming the pyramid's foundation. As each need is met, increasingly nuanced needs can be pursued—safety, belonging, esteem, and ultimately self-actualization. This framework was articulated by Abraham Maslow in *A Theory of Human Motivation*, written in 1943, and is illustrative of how we identify high-impact change.

MASLOW'S HIERARCHY OF HUMAN NEEDS
CHANGES THAT AFFECT THE BASE LEVELS HAVE BROAD EFFECTS

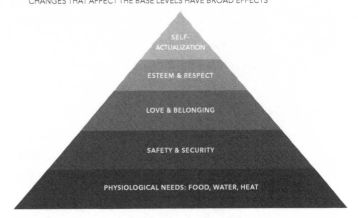

Source: A. H. Maslow, *A Theory of Human Motivation*, 1943.

When identifying catalysts, we are looking for the things that impact the bottom of the pyramid, which are the fundamental needs of humans. We think about elements such as food, energy, and water—existential requirements for human life across the spectrum of developed and developing nations. A new technology that has the potential to significantly impact the availability, delivery, and production mechanisms for food, for example, is something that we pay a great deal of attention to. Were that development to come to fruition, it would matter to everyone, everywhere. Similarly, technologies that have the potential to materially impact how we work, travel, and live are focus areas in our model. Markets and business systems are important, but changes to the underlying fabric of society that these systems sit on top of can be transformational far beyond the confines of a single industry.

We identify potential catalysts by assessing four primary factors: scope, magnitude, timing, and maturity. When evaluating technology specifically, we also look for a concentration of entrepreneurial talent and investment capital that make early-stage companies actionable as vendors or acquisition targets for larger organizations. Additionally, we look at the strategic landscape on which organizations operate in a holistic fashion, going beyond specific industry implications to identify connections between sectors and industries.

While we are not ready to declare Hyperloop technology the next great thing, let us look at the major advancements under way in this technology as an example of how we screen different types of technological developments. Hyperloop is a suite of technologies designed to transport people and cargo significantly faster and more cheaply than air travel. If Hyperloop were to be built with the capabilities that current design teams believe is possible, companies in the transportation industry would be affected, to be sure—but so would agriculture, energy, aerospace, retail, and manufacturing companies, as well as city, state, and national governments. It would matter to every industry without exception, as transportation and logistics are fundamental elements of all economic and governance systems. Even software and professional services companies would benefit from greater connectivity and lower transportation costs.

Certainly, there are a series of safety, affordability, regulatory, and technology challenges that need to be addressed before Hyperloop becomes commercially viable; however, it is a potential catalyst and must be evaluated in context of its potential global significance. The last major shift in transportation came more than half a century ago with broadly available commercial aviation. Since then, we have innovated to create better planes, cheaper travel, and more safety, but the transportation paradigm has remained largely unchanged. This is why we pay close attention to developments in this field.

Before a catalyst is completely visible, we tend to see signposts that allow us to know it is approaching. Many catalysts and subsequent transformations are a result of the convergence of a series of different technological and process innovations.

It is possible to track the individual elements that build toward a catalyst by disaggregating the overall trend and examining the parts. In doing so, you can identify the signposts that indicate the direction of a coming shift, and the potential tipping point represented by an emerging catalyst.

Genetic research is important, but the convergence of genomic technology, computer-enabled modeling and simulation, and biotechnology will be transformational. We do not presume to be able to predict the exact time that the developments converge to create a specific inflection point, but by disaggregating some of these themes, we can establish signposts and a framework to evaluate timing to facilitate better decisions by leaders.

For instance, we believe a catalyst is nearing in the area of renewable energy. There are three main areas that we believe are converging to constitute a significant change in this field, which we describe in more detail in a later chapter. These areas are grid storage technologies (batteries), whose progress can be measured by looking at energy density and storage cost-per-megawatt indicators; solar- and wind-generation technologies, which are measured by cost and efficiency curves; and the regulatory shift to revise the economic model for how energy is bought and sold, which involves a more qualitative monitoring of policy and commercial developments.

People will inevitably argue over the exact tipping point for each of these areas, but tracking their progress in a systematic way allows us to understand the directionality and speed of advance toward a transformational outcome.

TYPES OF CATALYSTS

The famous refrain about known knowns, known unknowns, and unknown unknowns is a useful framework to think broadly about other potential catalysts that can rapidly emerge and drive meaningful change. There are developments that we know and can monitor closely. There are fields where we see progress and suspect that a breakthrough could occur but are not sure which development approach will succeed, which we can also track. Then there are developments that come from areas we are not watching closely and may not see ahead of time. For these unknowns, our goal is to develop a framework to identify them as quickly as possible once they do start to become broadly relevant. By identifying our areas of exposure with a risk management framework, it becomes a more straightforward task to monitor and anticipate if and how unanticipated changes will impact different market segments.

Technology is critical, but not all catalysts are technology-driven. These are the types of catalysts that we have both seen historically and monitor today:

- Geopolitics and war
- Political and ideological movements

- Religious and broad social movements
- Health, famine, and disease
- Technology
- Ecological and environmental forces

HOW THE FAX MACHINE TOOK DOWN AN EMPIRE

It is very common for leaders to predict emerging catalysts but underestimate their full impact. For many years after World War II, the Soviet Union succeeded in building an empire through a system of blocked communication. They managed populations and satellite countries by controlling the information that went in and out of those countries, primarily by tapping phone lines and intercepting mail. Soviet propaganda teams spread disinformation and carefully controlled the education system to limit the information that people had access to. The underlying message behind their information campaign was simple: communism was a superior form of government, while capitalism made the lives of people miserable. But there was one source of information that they neither fully understood nor figured out how to control: the fax machine.

The resistance inside the Soviet Union used the fax machine to share secrets, organize, and communicate with the people inside and outside the Iron Curtain.[26] Thanks in part to the fax machine, the resistance in countries such as Czechoslovakia spread to East Germany, as they relayed information about protestors pouring across borders. Once the wall came down in Berlin, the information flow could no longer be curbed, and the disintegration of the Soviet Union accelerated rapidly. The fax machine—one simple invention—disrupted their monopoly on information, and they never recovered.

The Soviet strategy was based on assumptions built around currently existing technologies, which again illustrates the bias of projecting the present on future thinking. When a new technology changed the communications paradigm, the Soviets' strategy no longer provided the intended outcome. It took longer for them to adjust to the new paradigm than it did for the implications of that new paradigm to critically disrupt their operations.

THE RISK OF INACTION

As leaders, we tend to be very good at understanding our specific field or industry; however, it is more difficult to look outside the bounds of our traditional areas of focus. The media environment is not helpful in this regard. We are bombarded with breathless announcements about inevitable disruption and revolution. Clearly, we must to learn to differentiate between what is transformational and what is simply interesting, but we must also learn how to look outside of the fields in which we operate and are most comfortable. The likelihood of cross-industry disruptions will continue to increase, and organizations need a way to stay ahead of it as much as possible. Establishing that framework of prioritization through the lens of risk can allow your organization to filter through those announcements in a targeted and productive fashion. This process can be made more effective by maintaining a defensive analytic posture, evaluating developments under the assumption that your current strategy will at some point be challenged. This allows us to maintain a bias toward action, which provides agility in the face of change.

A broad view of the market helps to identify areas where further focus is required. But what happens if you do not have the skills or personnel to give the matter a closer look? Even in an organization with hundreds of thousands of employees, it is impossible to be an expert in everything. Technology moves too quickly and is often only truly understood by deep researchers in these fields. While it is undoubtedly important to create teams that can think broadly across a wide variety of emerging developments, at times one must look outside of one's organization in order to correlate strategy with emerging developments in peripheral industry.

Striking a balance between strategic and tactical views across an organization is crucial. Senior leaders tend to have a more strategic, thirty-thousand-foot view of everything happening across an industry, allowing them to observe big-picture developments at that high level. Line leaders tend to have a more tactical, ground-level view of how specific developments interact with key business processes. These views must be brought together, and each team member must be empowered to see the entire chessboard in context of existing strategy. A robust organizational view should connect emerging market or technological developments with forward-looking strategy to identify intersections that create opportunities or risks far enough in advance to allow the organization to adapt.

If you have gone through the risk management framework and identified areas where external change would have a magnified effect, you will be able to focus organizational energy where it can be most impactful. But again, it is important to note that you may need to look beyond the boundaries of your traditional industry to see what is happening in other industries and how those developments create risks for your organization. Although not all of the effects of a catalyst can be predicted, a proactive approach now can shield your organization from a great deal of future pain.

Catalysts affect the foundation on which we build strategy. Even the best and most well-implemented corporate strategies will fail if they are built on assumptions of future market conditions that prove to be incorrect. Similarly, even national strategy will fail if it is built on incorrect assumptions about the future geostrategic environment within which that nation operates.

LEADING YOUR ORGANIZATION INTO THE FUTURE

Throughout the second half of the book, we will assess some of the major opportunities and threats that have gathered over the past several decades in the areas of cities, demographics, manufacturing, power, and technology. These are catalysts that we believe are emerging and will disrupt both public and private sector organizations.

Our hope is that reading through each of the coming chapters—even if the immediate impact seems unrelated to your organization—may help you to begin to think about some of the major transformations to the global system that are emerging. Consider this a step toward impactful organizational growth.

The catalysts we focus on will enable new companies to emerge and will diminish, and in some cases destroy, companies we currently trust and respect. Some public sector institutions will be able to transform and provide excellent services and benefits to their charges, and others will be left behind in the wake of change, to the detriment of their citizens and constituents. We do not presume to have full knowledge of how these systems will evolve, but we are confident that these changes matter. We will have achieved our objective if we help spark awareness and thinking on these important topics.

5

MANUFACTURING

The increasing shift towards additive and autonomous manufacturing represents a fundamental shift to the way goods and structures are made. While a wholesale transition to additive manufacturing practices is still several decades off, even incremental adoption will impact the manufacturing industry—the backbone of globalization—in massive ways, bringing about huge shifts in global trade patterns and market dynamics.

LIKELIHOOD OF OCCURRENCE

IMPACT ON INDUSTRY

IMPACT ON THE PUBLIC SECTOR

AVAILABILITY OF SOLUTIONS

Manufacturing and the associated supply chains form the backbone of globalization. This is a somewhat obvious, but nonetheless important, concept. Manufacturing's fundamental role in globalization must underpin any discussion on future shifts in core manufacturing technologies and processes. Such shifts necessarily mean a corresponding shift in globalization and the structure of the global economy. The two subjects are inextricable.

The manufacturing process begins with materials that are created or extracted in one place, either from the environment or in a lab. Those materials are moved by truck, train, or ship, generally to a developing country where labor costs are low. There, they are manufactured into component parts, which tend to be less complex or lower value added in the parlance of economists. Multiple component parts from different regions are then moved to a second location—usually in a more developed country or region with the facilities and skilled labor to support more complex processes—where they are assembled into a more complex subcomponent. From there, these subcomponents are moved to a third, even more advanced assembly location where they are made into the end product that will be sold to customers. After assembly into the end product, these goods are then moved to where the customers are or to a distribution site where they can then be moved to retail or warehousing locations.

In some cases, this chain of events is simple, but in other cases, it can be incredibly complex, with numerous stops for manufacturing and assembly. In some cases, the process happens locally; in other cases, it can happen in different parts of the globe all at once.

Consider the laptop computer. A run-of-the-mill laptop could include a graphics processor made in Taiwan, CPU made in Arizona, hard drive made in Thailand, LCD made in South Korea, battery made in Japan, motherboard made in China or Mexico, RAM made in Idaho, and chipset made in Malaysia.[27] Before that, materials that any of these subcomponents are constructed out of could come from dozens of countries, creating a laptop that was partially built on every continent or, at a minimum, with materials that came from every continent (except Antarctica, for the time being).

This is the state of the global economy we live in today. The common understanding that products are manufactured where labor and materials are cheapest is correct, but the dynamic is far more complex than that understanding suggests. Economies of scale drive specialization across all categories of goods in a truly global system.

GLOBALIZATION AND TRADE
MASSIVE INCREASE IN GLOBAL TRADE VOLUME UNDERPINS GLOBALIZATION

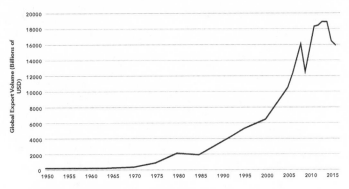

Source: "Statistics," United Nations Conference on Trade and Development, accessed January 22, 2018, http://unctad.org/en/Pages/statistics.aspx.

Due to this degree of complexity and interconnectivity, any significant change in the manufacturing process has broad impacts across the globe. Virtually all national economies are based on some balance of global manufacturing and consumption. Emerging transformations in the manufacturing field are centered on technological advances in additive manufacturing, the most common application of which is 3D printing. 3D printing technologies and processes are in the process of fundamentally disrupting the manufacturing sector. This disruption will cascade through shipping, logistics, transportation, infrastructure, construction, retail, and aerospace companies; it will also impact governments, national economies, and labor in both developed and developing countries.

To drastically oversimplify, traditional manufacturing

is based on *subtraction*. The manufacturer begins with a block of material from which they cut away whatever is not needed for the final product. The computer numeric control (CNC) machine, which is present in virtually every manufacturing plant in the world, makes cuts to raw materials to create the product's parts. Due to the way CNC and other traditional manufacturing machines work, they will always leave some type of waste material.

3D printing, by contrast, operates on an additive model of manufacturing. 3D printing starts with a base material and builds up layers until the completed object is created. While 3D printing is currently viewed by the general public primarily as a hobbyist tool, it is important to understand that the widespread adoption of these technologies into core manufacturing processes is far more important than another incremental development that will simply reduce costs or streamline existing manufacturing processes. It is a fundamentally different way of building everything, and it has the very real potential to upend the global system.

TRENDS

Additive manufacturing technologies have advanced over the past thirty years to incorporate increasingly complex materials and structures, from plastics to metals and organic compounds. The technology is not new; it traces back to stereolithography, which was the starting point in the 1980s that gave rise to the low-cost 3D printers that came to market in the late 1990s and early 2000s. In the 2010s, the demand and variety of use cases for 3D printing systems has increased significantly. The current environment reflects the culmination of thirty years of technological development—progress that has largely been unnoticed by the general public until recently.

Thus far, 3D printing technologies have seen widespread integration into prototyping and niche low-rate production areas—specifically, those that use expensive materials and where the cost of material waste is high. One example of this is the aerospace industry, which uses incredibly expensive materials such as titanium to build select structural components. The use cases for this technology are accelerating in propagation in many industries and around the globe.

Currently, 3D printing represents about 0.04 percent of the global manufacturing market and less than 1 percent of all goods manufactured in the United States. Wohlers Associates, a leading expert in the field, estimates that the additive manufacturing industry has experienced around a 26 percent compound annual growth rate over the past twenty-seven years. It generated $6.1 billion in 2016, up from $4 billion in 2013. There were forty-nine companies producing and selling additive manufacturing systems in 2014, sixty-two in 2015, and ninety-seven in

2016.[28] An industry-wide survey conducted by Sculpteo in 2015 reported that 68 percent of respondents planned to increase spending on additive manufacturing in the next year. Top uses for 3D printing in 2015 were functional parts (29 percent), fit-and-finish components (18 percent), molds and tooling (10 percent), and visual proofs of concept (10 percent), demonstrating a clear transition toward more holistic applications.[29]

3D PRINTING
PROJECTED 2020 GLOBAL UNIT SHIPMENTS OF 3D PRINTERS

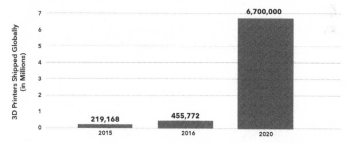

Source: "Gartner Says Worldwide Shipments of 3D Printers to Grow 108 Percent in 2016," Newsroom, Gartner, October 13, 2016, https://www.gartner.com/newsroom/id/3476317.

The applications of 3D printing are becoming more and more diverse. The medical device industry is one example of an industry that is already changing significantly because of 3D printing technology. In 2015, 98 percent of all hearing aids worldwide were manufactured using 3D printing.[30] The technology allows a doctor to take precise measurements of a person's ear and construct aids that uniquely fit a customer's specific anatomy. In addition to hearing aids, the medical device industry currently uses 3D printing for orthodontic implants and surgical guides. This will soon expand into stents and prosthetics that can be more easily and cost-efficiently customized on an individual basis.

The automotive industry currently uses 3D printing for specialized components and prototype/concept car designs. Companies such as AutoZone, one of the largest American auto part manufacturers, are exploring how they can take advantage of 3D printing. In the near future, entire chassis may be printed, providing lighter-weight, more robust designs with fewer stress points. In the longer term, more complex multipart additive manufacturing techniques will allow more of the vehicle structure to be printed, which would lower costs and increase the ability to customize smaller production runs.

Consumer products companies currently use 3D printing in limited applications for niche goods, such as custom jewelry and high-end sporting goods. In the near future, companies will be able to manufacture apparel and accessories using this technology, providing for a wider range of customization and personalization.

An interesting longer-term application is in the growing commercial space business. Long-haul space missions will require a way for astronauts to produce their own supplies. Developing systems that can 3D print objects in a zero-gravity or micro-gravity environment has presented a challenge, but the potential benefit to future space travel is immense: the material used in the printer packs neatly in blocks and takes up less space and less weight than traditional supply packs. The cost savings will come in to the tune of hundreds of thousands of dollars per launch.

People are currently printing everything from full-scale houses and body parts to multiform objects that change shape when a current is introduced. These developments are all important to their respective industries, but we believe the true catalyst inflection point is when technological advancements and adoption rates converge to make 3D printing central to mainstream process as opposed to selective or niche applications.

More and more applications are being discovered, and the displacement resulting from 3D printing that we are already starting to see will become more prevalent over time. The inflection point will emerge when more traditional large-scale factory manufacturing processes transition from injection molding and other techniques to 3D printing. As we have discussed, we believe this transition represents a global catalyst, which will have effects that extend far beyond the manufacturing sector. The technologies are important on their own, but because manufacturing is the backbone of globalization, they stand to affect the global geopolitical landscape and virtually everyone who lives and works in the integrated global economy.

THE REGIONALIZATION OF ECONOMIC ACTIVITY

The continued development and eventual widespread adoption of 3D printing will change the shape of global trade. A significant portion of global trade is predicated on the lowest-cost manufacturing model, where simple items (door hinges and widgets) and subcomponents for more complex products (iPhones) are produced wherever they can be made most cheaply, then shipped to an assembly facility or directly to consumer markets. As with the typical laptop computer, the supply chains for these items can involve dozens of different stops around the world.

In general, additive manufacturing will decrease the cost variance between manufacturing some categories of items locally and in faraway markets with lower labor costs. If manufacturing costs for printing an item locally or overseas are the same, the locally printed item will be cheaper because the transportation cost to get that item to the end customer or assembly factory will be lower. Economics will drive companies to shift manufacturing from low labor-cost countries to manufacturing centers as close as possible to the end customer.

Accordingly, we expect to see more localized or regionalized manufacturing, even in developed markets. This is critical, as the movement of goods from low production-cost markets to end-customer markets underpins globalization. If globalization is measured by the volume of global trade, this metric is almost certain to decline in an environment where it becomes a cost advantage for many categories of industrial goods to 3D print them locally.

In 2013, it was estimated that around 90 percent of all the goods we buy arrive via ship. That shipping volume represents around 2 percent of global GDP, more than the contribution of restaurants, takeaway food, and civil engineering combined.[31] Shipping companies require high volumes of goods shipped to maintain low prices. With a smaller base of items being transported to spread those costs over, per-unit shipping costs will be higher. As such, we anticipate that once some companies begin to onshore enough manufacturing to affect shipping patterns, shipping costs will rise.

Higher per-unit shipping costs will incentivize other companies to adopt additive manufacturing technologies so they can localize their manufacturing to avoid more expensive shipping costs. This will result in a fundamental downward spiral for shipping companies that will serve to incentivize a more rapid adoption of additive manufacturing processes than would be the case without the shipping cost dynamic.

If 3D printing ultimately results in a decline of global trade volume, the effects become far more widespread. It is not only the shipping industry that will be affected; in fact, every leader of an organization in any industry should understand the technology's potential to fundamentally alter shipping, logistics, manufacturers, retailers, job creation, and international trade.

Widespread adoption of 3D printing will generally be positive for developed economies as they transition from global to more local supply chains. Manufacturing and retail companies within those economies will be more capital efficient. Trade balances will shift in favor of fewer foreign imports. New jobs will be created to support additive manufacturing facilities. These will not be traditional manufacturing jobs, nor will they be created at a volume high enough to entirely replace prior manufacturing job losses; however, this catalyst will create new and different types of manufacturing jobs in developed economies.

Conversely, the widespread adoption of 3D printing will generally be negative for those countries that previously manufactured goods that will now be produced in developed countries, nearer to the point of sale. The economic advantage of manufacturing some categories of goods in low-cost manufacturing areas will cease to exist or be drastically reduced. Some developing economies will be able to shift focus toward other forms of primary activity, but others will not, and the competition for remaining low-end manufacturing activity will increase, with corresponding downward pressure on the cost of labor.

Companies that build and sell things that can be 3D printed in part or in whole will benefit from cheaper manufacturing costs; those that move things and provide logistics capacity will be negatively impacted by shrinking demand. Shipping companies specifically will face significant challenges unless the decreases in aggregate manufacturing-related shipping demand are replaced with new categories of other items needing transport. Infrastructure and construction companies will benefit from different material construction techniques, as will aerospace companies and vehicle manufacturers.

MANUFACTURING AND GLOBAL SECURITY DYNAMICS

While every country's path toward development has its own nuances and unique components, there are some common features among countries that have developed over the past several hundred years. Quite simply, most countries start their development by manufacturing low-end goods and subcomponents that are shipped to more developed countries, which then integrate them into finished products. Countries then build on this foundation of low-end manufacturing to move up the value chain.

After low-end subcomponents, countries gradually start to manufacture higher-end parts and finished goods, which facilitates domestic consumption and a virtuous cycle that leads to a higher value-added economy.

The United States followed this path by producing spun cotton in the South and industrial goods in the North during its development in the eighteenth and nineteenth centuries. China followed this path in recent years by manufacturing a number of low-end goods that support a variety of markets. This is an extremely common development path and is how the majority of today's first world economies were able to develop. There are some exceptions for countries that have been able to leverage their natural resources, such as oil, to skip the low-end manufacturing phase and emerge directly as higher value-added economies, but these exceptions are rare.

If the 3D printing industry continues to mature, it is possible that it will no longer be economically efficient to outsource manufacturing of low-end goods and subcomponents. Those items will be fabricated in 3D printing factories near their end customers. Developed economies will enjoy cheaper finished goods and more jobs, but the consequences for developing economies could be disastrous.

It is unclear what will happen if developing economies are not able to progress via this traditional method. They may find other routes toward development to circumvent the lack of opportunity in the low-end manufacturing space. Another possible outcome is that these economies simply will not develop, remaining outside of and likely disenfranchised by the global economic system. This is unfortunate on the human level, but it also presents a general security concern. Isolation creates an incentive—potentially an imperative—for those countries to disrupt the system that has left them behind.

3D PRINTING AND THE PRIVATE SECTOR

At their most basic level, 3D printing technologies enable customization at scale, which facilitates new design paradigms and stands to improve the consumer product experience immensely. If companies no longer have to mass produce identical items at scale in order to drive down costs, custom products will become economically competitive for the first time since the small-town tailor and craftsman. Companies are and will be able to manufacture apparel and accessories using these technologies, providing for a wider range of customization and personalization. This could manifest as individualized designs and as custom-fitted artifacts designed for an individual's unique measurements, both of which could be produced at scale using 3D printing technologies.

In fact, we are already seeing consumer products companies using 3D printing in limited applications for niche goods such as custom jewelry and high-end sporting goods. A 3D printed jacket was introduced in 2017 by Israeli designer Danit Peleg, marketed as "the first 3D printed garment ever sold online."[32] We are on the cusp of a new explosion in creativity, with companies being able to customize fashion, furniture, housing, and other basic goods directly to the consumer's needs and best fit. This is not a one-off custom system per se but rather represents customization at scale, including individuals being able to directly design and manufacture some goods themselves.

When we apply the principle of customization at scale to the individual, we also anticipate the revival of the craftsman, or craftsperson. A 3D printer is relatively inexpensive, hardware-wise, and the computer aided design (CAD) software required to run it is highly accessible and has been used by engineers for years. Think back to the 1980s when home computers made it possible for a whole new generation to learn ways to creatively program their own software tools and games. The designers and coders who unleashed multibillion-dollar companies started with their home computers as teenagers. Imagine what we might do in our economy when highly capable and broadly accessible 3D printing applications unleash a new generation of inventors and designers. The similar innovation and entrepreneurial energy that has been applied to software development can be translated into physical goods at scale via additive manufacturing technologies.

Additive manufacturing will also enable more efficient "just-in-time" inventory management processes, as opposed to traditional warehousing and distribution systems. There is an entire sector built around inventory management and anticipating what organizations may need at a given time. Simply stated, the current common practice for many American companies is to design an item, have tens of thousands of units manufactured in China, ship them to the United States, and warehouse them until they are sold. In the current subtractive manufacturing environment, both manufacturing and shipping costs go up significantly if companies order smaller production runs, and it is difficult to react quickly to customer demand because of the time delay involved in ship transit across the Pacific Ocean.

Additive manufacturing could enable some types of goods to be produced on demand, at similar cost to a large production run, reducing or eliminating the need to maintain a large network of warehouses. This would be significant to the companies and real estate investors that support warehousing and could enable the growth of new types of inventory management companies and products.

While we have already discussed the impact of 3D printing

on globalization, it is important to reflect specifically on what this means for the shipping and logistics industry, as many other types of companies rely on this industry. Manufactured goods make up 15 to 25 percent of total global shipping volume, and some percentage of those manufactured goods could be fabricated closer to the end customer.[33] It stands to reason that shipping demand will decrease as a result of this technology. And because the shipping industry operates at a high fixed-to-variable cost ratio, even a marginal decrease in volume could have a magnified effect.

As mentioned previously, shipping is a capital-intensive industry, and large cargo ships are expensive. The cost for the ship is spread across each item it transports. Currently, the cost to ship an item is historically inexpensive, in part because the volume of items shipped is high. If the industry suffers a major decrease in demand, it will lead to overcapacity, and shipping costs will rise because the same (fixed) costs of the ships will be spread over a smaller base of items shipped. Higher prices could cause other companies to search for local solutions, which could create a slippery slope effect that would severely constrain these businesses.

Let us consider a recent event to illustrate the point that financial difficulties within the shipping and logistics industry can have far-reaching impacts. In February 2017, the Hanjin shipping company out of Korea went bankrupt while at sea. They had shipments stuck outside of the Los Angeles ports system without being allowed to dock because no one would underwrite the costs that the shipping company owed but could not pay. The ports essentially used the shipped merchandise as collateral that might recover some of what they were owed.

While the shipping company scrambled to find a solution, major American retail companies, who likely did not know they were exposed to the dynamics of the shipping industry, felt the crunch while their expected products sat on a boat instead of making their way to distribution centers. Some eighty to ninety vessels were scattered worldwide, holding five hundred thousand containers that represented $14 billion in merchandise.[34] This is another piece of evidence that we no longer have the luxury of focusing on the dynamics of only our own industries. Shifts and challenges have far-reaching consequences.

Another interesting consequence to consider for the private sector is that additive manufacturing will likely increase the relative value of things that cannot be 3D printed. In recent decades, we have witnessed a remarkable decrease in the cost of easily manufactured goods and commodities. This will accelerate with the widespread adoption of additive manufacturing technologies. In a world of increasing abundance, it is not difficult to imagine handmade goods and services being more highly valued and driving corresponding price premiums.

3D PRINTING AND THE PUBLIC SECTOR

There are several levels at which these shifts affect decision making for public sector leaders. To begin with the strategic implications, leaders at all levels need to pursue a proactive and deliberate approach to managing the transition from the current to the future global manufacturing environment. The shift toward additive manufacturing technologies will be accompanied, to some degree, by an increasing regionalization of economic activity, which affects a variety of economic planning and development activities.

This will not happen overnight, nor is it a binary shift where the economy is either global or regional. But it is critical to realize that even a seemingly minor shift to the distribution of economic activity can be important and should be planned for. Economic planning occurs at the city, state, and national levels, and leaders at all these levels have the responsibility to prepare their regions and constituents for these shifts. In many of the more developed parts of the world that stand to benefit the most from this transition, planning considerations will focus on infrastructure investments, education considerations, and import/export tax policy.

In developing nations that depend on the low-value added types of manufacturing that could be displaced as a result of the increasing adoption of additive manufacturing technologies, the challenge is more difficult. If, after a more detailed evaluation, leaders believe that they are at risk of suffering a significant economic downturn if manufacturing demand were to decrease, the response would be to explore a policy of economic diversification to mitigate the impacts of retraction in any specific sector. However, this is much more easily said than done, especially in an environment of limited investment capital for new types of training and facilities.

Additive manufacturing can help immensely with poverty in developing nations if incorporated thoughtfully—in a regionalized manufacturing environment, even poor nations will need to develop regional economies. By lowering the capital requirements and barriers to entry for manufacturing, continued advances in 3D printing creates new opportunities for small businesses to make diversified groups of products and develop design intellectual property that can be sold in the global marketplace. A small business owner in Nairobi, Kenya, may not have the capital to secure the specialized equipment designed for mass manufacturing, but they could invest in 3D printers to support their local markets with the locally produced goods.

At the more tactical level, regulatory bodies must stay

ahead of these innovations. National and international regulatory bodies such as the Occupational Safety and Health Administration (OSHA) and the International Organization for Standardization (ISO) will face significant challenges to apply old regulatory frameworks to new environments. Done correctly, regulators would work hand in hand with innovators to ensure that logical and responsible safety standards are applied without inhibiting the pace of innovation. Unfortunately, this is rarely the case, and some of the pioneers of 3D printing are already struggling against what they believe is an archaic regulatory environment that lacks any real direction.

The fears are twofold: either an unsupervised landscape will lead to a health and safety disaster and corresponding regulatory backlash, or the government will step in and issue regulations without a full understanding of the technology and what aspects actually should be regulated. There are also public safety concerns about the ability for people to design and 3D manufacture items currently prohibited in some countries, such as firearms. You could imagine a new role for the public sector to think about ways to control the production of weapon systems that can now be created in a garage without the specialized equipment that was previously needed. The regulatory sector's role in this shift will be to facilitate benefits for the economy while setting the standards as a trusted organization.

SOLUTIONS

Innovation leads to change, which leads to unpredictability and uncertainty. Businesses and governments, now more than ever, must remain flexible. Leaders should be open to thinking about their core assets—products, manufacturing, supply chains, and logistics—in different ways.

Logistics companies may rethink the capital structures and finance versus buying decisions they currently make to run the business, such as how much of a shipping fleet a company wants to own as a fixed asset cost as opposed leasing ships. The latter approach, for example, may require business leaders to sacrifice margin in the near term in order to provide the flexibility to mitigate an uncertain—but potentially catastrophic—longer-term outcome. These are difficult decisions both to make and to communicate to investors and employees, especially when operating in public markets.

Public sector leaders should not assume each new technology will simply slide into an existing regulatory framework. They must understand and appreciate the uniqueness of each application, identifying where it does and does not need its own set of rules. Striking the right balance between maintaining an appropriate regulatory posture and allowing further innovation is crucial for technology to succeed.

As this catalyst continues to evolve, it will unlock the

imaginations of artisans, hobbyists, young people, and craftsmen in a way that we have not seen since the personal home computer hit the market. Bill Gates and his contemporaries changed the world because of the opportunities they had as teenagers with home computers, learning code and imagining the possibilities. It is exciting to envision what today's young adults will be able to accomplish when they can push a button and see their ideas built. They can tinker and experiment, design and redesign until the next revolutionary products and solutions emerge. Consider how the story of *Apollo 13* may have unfolded differently if there were a 3D printer on board. It is not much of a stretch to anticipate a Mars colony that uses locally sourced materials and a 3D printer to sustain itself; in fact, additive manufacturing may prove to be one of the key innovations that makes new forms of exploration possible.

The military is another potentially transformational use case. Military depots will clearly benefit from the just-in-time capabilities provided by a global network of 3D printers, but consider how these technologies could change the very nature of military operations. A famous military maxim states: "Amateurs study tactics; professionals study logistics." It takes a mountain of supplies to support an army during an operation. We are not far away from 3D printing developing to a point where armies deploy with the capability to fabricate key rapidly consumable supplies at the front lines, eliminating a huge part of the traditional military supply trains.

In the twenty-seven days following D-Day—the American invasion of Normandy on June 6, 1944—566,548 tons of supplies and 171,532 vehicles were poured into Normandy to support the invasion.[35] It took years for Allied logisticians to prepare and pre-position these supplies. What would it mean if a future invading force could simply drop shipping-container-sized fabrication units to build these supplies? Or for the infantry company to print supplies inside a patrol base behind enemy lines? How does this affect military decision making? Does it lower or raise the decision calculus for countries that want to pursue military operations against their neighbors? While these capabilities will undoubtedly enable humanitarian relief efforts, what will they mean in the hands of revisionist powers and violent extremist organizations?

As with all technologies, these developments are not inherently good or bad; they simply are and must be understood and adjusted to. There will be dividing lines between the business and government actors that make this adjustment successfully and those that do not. With respect to developing economies, it is in everyone's interest to mitigate a growing gap between the haves and have-nots and to enable broad participation in the next wave of technology and innovation. We continue to see the results of political elections, revisionist ideologies, and reactionary policies when people feel technology is making their lives worse. Imagine the implications of this trend on a larger global scale among emerging nations more broadly. The world is changing, and while there is no guarantee that all these changes will be positive, they must be managed thoughtfully and proactively.

POWER

Advances in battery technology are enabling renewables to become economically viable without government subsidies. This creates a shift in global energy dynamics; renewable energy facilitates the localization of power production and consumption, and stands to change the shape of energy markets in both developed and developing countries. While renewables will not universally replace hydrocarbon-based power generation, it is important to remember that the last major shift in primary energy technology—coal to oil— changed the world.

LIKELIHOOD OF OCCURRENCE

IMPACT ON INDUSTRY

IMPACT ON THE PUBLIC SECTOR

AVAILABILITY OF SOLUTIONS

Because of the foundational nature of the relationship between society and power, any significant changes to energy availability and power generation technologies can have far-reaching impacts. While a technological advance leading to 10 percent greater efficiency for internal combustion engines would be important and would alter the competitive landscape within the transportation industry, we would view that as an incremental advancement within the current transportation paradigm.

However, a shift to a new primary power source or type of power generation technology would constitute a transformation with far-reaching effects beyond the bounds of the energy industry. We believe that a catalyst is emerging in the broad category of renewable energy, primarily focused on solar and wind power.

While renewables have been talked about as the next great energy source for decades, these technologies are now nearing the point where they are economically viable when compared to traditional energy sources on a non-subsidized basis. That inflection point—when renewable power becomes cheaper than traditional power sources on a real basis—will not only impact the companies that operate in the energy and natural resource industries but other industries and public institutions that rely on energy as well.

This inflection point is rapidly approaching, and the key development that will enable this transformation is battery technology. There are three different areas that must converge in order for renewables to be economically viable. The first is the cost, reliability, and efficiency of solar and wind power generation technology. The second are efficient grid-storage batteries to offset the load leveling issue. For example, there is a need to balance times of highest solar power generation (day) with highest use (night). The third is a business model and regulatory issue, as the current economic framework will need to be adjusted to accommodate the new technologies, which we will discuss in further detail.

These developments are happening now. In some parts of the United States, renewables are already at or below cost parity with traditional power generation. However, the transition in primary power generation technologies will be gradual, because even when power generation costs reach parity between renewables and hydrocarbons. The latter will remain the lower-cost option in some cases because of the sunk costs in infrastructure investments that developed countries have made over the past generations. Renewables must become significantly cheaper if they are to overcome those switching costs.

RELATIVE POWER GENERATION COSTS

UNSUBSIDIZED GENERATION COST IN THE US PER KWH
2016 LOW-TO-HIGH ESTIMATES

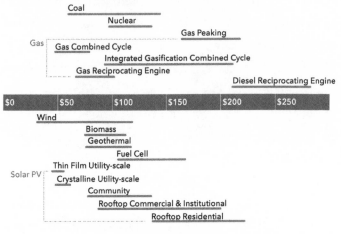

Source: "Levelized Cost of Energy Analysis 10.0," Lazard Estimates and BNEF (December 15, 2016), https://www.lazard.com/perspective/levelized-cost-of-energy-analysis-100/.

Even after taking the switching costs into account, we are approaching the inflection point. Solar and wind is now the same price or cheaper than fossil fuels in more than thirty countries, according to the World Economic Forum.[36] This transition is broadly relevant, because our energy needs impact everything in our world, from the way we move, to the physical footprint of our towns and cities, how much discretionary income we need to spend on it, how our food is produced and transported to us, and how we keep our bodies and our communities healthy.

Once this transformation occurs, its effects will be significant. We anticipate meaningful shifts to industry dynamics, including the view of real estate as a productive asset class, important changes to the shapes and possibilities for cities, new opportunities for developing nations, and global trade and geopolitics. Because of the foundational role of energy in society, any significant shift to the current paradigm will represent a catalyst with far-reaching effects.

While energy storage technologies and electric vehicles are a critical part of this transformation, we are focusing this discussion on residential, commercial, and industrial energy consumption, which constitutes the bulk of energy used in the United States. According to the US Energy Information Administration (EIA),[37] 29 percent of US energy was used for transportation in 2016, with the remaining 71 percent consumed in residential, commercial, and industrial applications. Electric vehicles benefit from these storage technologies, but power generation technologies and economic issues are more directly focused on non-transportation uses.

TRENDS

Renewable energy is a broad category that encompasses power generated from the sun, wind, geothermal heat, biomass, tides, rivers, and other sources. As with all energy applications, power must be generated, moved to the point of consumption, and consumed as electricity. The importance of storage varies based on the type of power generation technology and the distance between the point of generation and the point of consumption.

These are not new technologies. Solar photovoltaic systems were implemented in the United States as early as the 1970s. Wind power has been harnessed since the age of sail, and windmills were used for power generation in the nineteenth century. Electrochemical batteries were developed the late eighteenth century and commercialized in the early nineteenth century. These technologies are now maturing rapidly and are nearing a low enough cost and high enough level of efficiency to become commercially viable, even when compared to coal, gas, and nuclear power.

To provide a baseline for our discussion on different types of power generation technologies, most US electricity is generated using fossil fuels. In the United States in 2016, according to the EIA, natural gas was the source of about 34 percent of electricity generation. Coal was the second largest energy source, constituting about 30 percent of all electricity generation. Petroleum is also used for electricity generation in diesel-engine generators but was the source of less than 1 percent of the total. Nuclear power provided about 20 percent of total electricity generation. The remaining 15 percent of US electricity was generated by renewable energy sources in 2016. Of these renewables, 6.5 percent was hydropower, 5.6 percent was wind, 1.5 percent was biomass, 0.9 percent was solar, and 0.4 percent was geothermal.

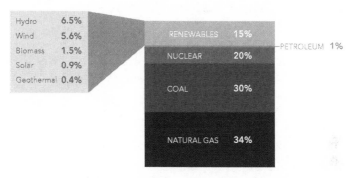

SOURCES OF US ELECTRICITY GENERATION IN 2016
THE MAJORITY OF US ELECTRICITY IS GENERATED BY FOSSIL FUELS

Hydro	6.5%
Wind	5.6%
Biomass	1.5%
Solar	0.9%
Geothermal	0.4%

RENEWABLES 15%

PETROLEUM 1%

NUCLEAR 20%

COAL 30%

NATURAL GAS 34%

Source: "Electricity Explained: Electricity in the United States," US Energy Information Administration, updated May 10, 2017, https://www.eia.gov/energyexplained/index.cfm?page=electricity_in_the_united_states.

The primary measurement for large-scale power generation is the gigawatt (GW), which represents 1,000 megawatts (MW). For reference, 1 GW is considered to power between 700,000–1,000,000 homes.[38] The typical coal power plant is considered be about 500 MW. A typical nuclear power plant has around a 2 GW capacity, with the largest plant in the United States being the Palo Verde plant in Arizona, with a combined generating capacity of its three reactors being just under 4 GW.

SOLAR POWER

The key component for solar power generation is the

photovoltaic cell (PV), which is a panel that converts light into electricity. There are different types of PV cells and different arrangements that can use lenses and mirrors to focus large areas of sunlight into tight beams, but the core PV technology has been used for decades.

Since early implementation in the 1970s and 1980s, costs have drastically decreased and efficiency has significantly increased, making solar a much more compelling technology. The solar industry has undergone remarkable growth in the last decade, due to both efficiency increases and cost reductions of PV cells. The global solar PV capacity has grown from around 5 GW in 2005 to approximately 230 GW in 2015.

In 2006, it cost $9 per watt of power generated by solar panels. As of 2015, that figure had dropped to approximately $3.79 per watt, and to around $3.57 per watt as of late 2016.[39] The average cost of standard 6 KW solar home system—without subsidies—fell from $52,920 to $20,160 in the past decade.[40] The very first solar cells were less than 1 percent efficient, as defined by the portion of sunlight that is converted to energy. By 1960, PV cells had achieved around 14 percent efficiency, which increased to 17.8 percent in 2012. Since then, the gains have increased rapidly. By 2015, Solar City, Panasonic, and Sun City all achieved over 22 percent efficiency. In January 2016, the National Renewable Energy Laboratory announced it had achieved 29.8 percent efficiency. Continuing efficiency gains will reduce the cost and increase the commercial viability of solar power.

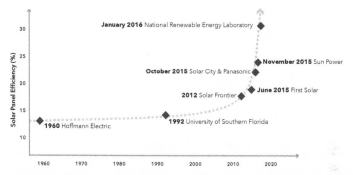

SOLAR POWER EFFICIENCY
SIGNIFICANT GAINS IN PV EFFICIENCY IN THE PAST 5 YEARS

Source: Sara Matasci, "How Solar Panel Cost and Efficiency Have Changed Over Time," Energy Sage, March 16, 2017, https://news.energysage.com/solar-panel-efficiency-cost-over-time/.

According to the Solar Energy Industries Association, the US-based solar industry has grown at a 60 percent compound annual growth rate over the past ten years. It employed nearly 374,000 Americans in 2016, up 25 percent from 2015.[41] This is more than work in coal, gas, and nuclear energy combined, although it is still less than 20 percent of the size of the workforce of Walmart.

The consumer applications are significantly increasing in functionality and versatility and decreasing in cost. As of February 2016, more than one million homes in the United States have installed solar panels. According to the Solar Energy Industry Association,[42] the United States added 125 solar panels per minute in 2016, around twice the rate of 2015. New consumer-friendly applications are emerging, such as Tesla's Solar Roof product that looks remarkably like a normal roof and will be durable enough to be warrantied for the life of a house.[43]

We commonly think of solar in terms of residential or small-scale commercial applications, but it is important to note that there are already significant concentrated solar power generation facilities in operation. Two facilities in California—the Desert Sunlight Solar Farm near the Mojave Desert and the Topaz Solar Farm near San Luis Obispo—both have a capacity of around 550 MW. The Tengger Desert Solar Park in the Inner Mongolia region of China, also known as the Great Wall of Solar, has a projected capacity of over 1.5 GW.

The commercial and industrial applications of solar power extend far beyond large, government-funded solar plants. One of the key benefits of solar, which we will discuss in further detail, is that it can be built at different scales without sacrificing the economics significantly. Small generation facilities, or even panels on rooftops or above parking lots, can generate power in a cost-efficient fashion.

While solar PV technology is mature, it is obviously dependent on the availability of sunlight, so solar power is not a universally applicable solution. As with wind and other renewables, these technologies are best viewed as part of a holistic energy solution that includes both renewables and fossil fuels.

GLOBAL SOLAR PV AND WIND CAPACITY
CUMULATIVE INSTALLED SOLAR PV AND WIND CAPACITY IS GROWING SIGNIFICANTLY

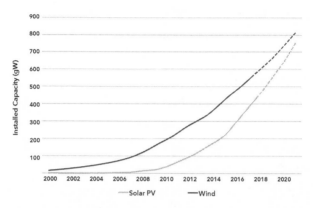

Source: "Global Wind Report, Annual Market Update 2016," Global Wind Energy Council, Accessed February 2018, http://gwec.net/.

"Global Market Outlook for Solar Power, 2017–2021," SolarPower Europe, Accessed February 2018, http://www.solarpowereurope.org.

WIND POWER

Wind power generation has also experienced significant growth in recent decades. The basic technology involved is the wind turbine. Wind turbines are grouped together into wind farms, which can range from dozens to thousands of turbines. The largest wind farm in the world is the Gansu Wind Farm in China, which has a projected generation capacity of 10 GW when complete via around seven thousand turbines. The Alta Wind Energy Center in California is the largest wind farm in the United States, with a 1.5 GW generation capacity.

The global installed capacity of wind power generation grew from approximately 59 GW in 2005 to 432 GW in 2015, according to the Global Wind Energy Council (GWEC). As of 2015, the largest country by cumulative wind generation capacity was China, with 33.6 percent of global wind generation capacity, followed by the United States at 17.2 percent and Germany at 10.4 percent.[44]

While the vast preponderance of wind generation facilities are on land, offshore wind generation tripled in capacity from 2011 to 2015. Although offshore generation accounted for only 12 GW in 2015, primarily in the United Kingdom and Germany, it represents an emerging area of innovation and development.

The cost of wind power has dropped by an average of 7 percent per year since 1985, comprising an overall cost reduction of over 90 percent during that period. Wind is increasingly becoming an important part of the power generation mix, especially in Europe. Denmark satisfies approximately 40 percent of its electricity demand via wind power. It has a 20 percent penetration in Portugal, Spain, and Ireland and has reached 5.6 percent in the United States. Remarkably, wind accounts for nearly 45 percent of the electrical power in Texas during peak conditions.[45]

Technological advances in both blade and tower design and materials sciences have provided for efficiency gains and cost reductions for wind power. At the simplest level, taller towers are more productive and allow greater geographic coverage of onshore wind turbines. Capacity factor, which reflects the fraction of the year that a turbine is operating at peak power (average output/peak output), is the most common measurement of turbine efficiency. The capacity factor for US wind projects increased from 31.2 percent during 2004–2011 to 41.2 percent in 2014, and it is continuing to increase.[46] General advances in manufacturing and construction technology and techniques benefit the wind power industry directly, as do materials that allow for lighter turbines—all of which will continue to increase the economic viability of wind-based power generation technologies.

BATTERY TECHNOLOGY AND GRID STORAGE SYSTEMS

Our discussion of solar and wind technologies was intended to demonstrate that these technologies are mature. On a pure power generation basis, wind and solar cost about the same to generate as does gas, coal, and nuclear power, as depicted in the graph regarding relative power costs earlier in this chapter. Battery technology is the remaining piece of the puzzle for the mainstream economic viability of renewables. A power storage solution is needed to offset the inherent variability of renewables that depend on sun or wind. When storage solutions become cost-efficient at scale, we can anticipate a dramatic increase in the fundamental economics and use of renewables. Current grid storage battery technology has historically not been efficient or cost-effective enough to enable renewables to truly compete with traditional energy production.

This is all about to change, thanks to significant advances in battery technology. Batteries are the critical path toward the significant expansion of renewable energy production and use. Rapid advances in this field have occurred over the past five years because of electric vehicles, which have created an important incentive for large companies to invest heavily in battery technology. Companies such as Tesla and others have invested billions in battery research to increase the range and performance of electric cars. Until this economic incentive was introduced, battery research had been relegated to "special project" status within companies and research institutions. This is not to say that battery research was considered unimportant, but now that advances in battery technology determine the success of important companies in as large an addressable market as automobiles, resources have surged into the field.

Batteries are the key constraint to both the economic viability of renewable power generation and the consumer acceptance of electric vehicles. Decreases in cost and increases in efficiency will allow more cost-effective energy storage systems for the home and the grid and will allow electric vehicles to travel farther per charge. The measurement we use for the cost efficiency of batteries is cost per kilowatt hour (kWh). A watt-hour is the amount of electricity that is consumed by a circuit using 1 watt of power for one hour, and is the same measurement we see on light bulbs and household utilities.

Both public and private sector research efforts have resulted in significant increases to battery efficiency. According to Bloomberg New Energy Finance, the average battery pack price across the industry has decreased from around $1,000/kWh in 2010 to $227/kWh in 2016, a 77 percent decline. These costs are projected to decline even further to $190/kWh by the end of the decade and below $100/kWh by 2030.[47]

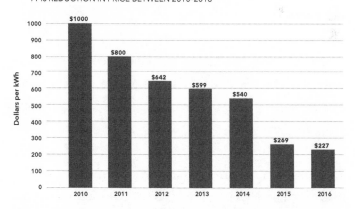

AVERAGE BATTERY PACK PRICE
77% REDUCTION IN PRICE BETWEEN 2010-2016

Source: "Electrifying Insights: How Automakers Can Drive Electrified Vehicle Sales and Profitability," Bloomberg New Energy Finance, McKinsey & Company, January 2017, https://www.mckinsey.de/files/161223_mckinsey_e-vehicles.pdf.

Tesla is ahead of this trend. In 2008, Tesla's batteries cost around $690/kWh, well below the industry average even a decade ago. On an analyst call in April 2016, a Tesla executive reported that their costs were already below $190/kWh, significantly ahead of the industry average.[48] Tesla's Gigafactory, which we mentioned previously, is designed to further reduce these costs by 35 percent once operational, so we may see further significant decreases in the near future. Many industry analysts project that a price point around $150/kWh will have a galvanizing effect, incentivizing broad adoption of both electric vehicles and grid storage systems.

Bloomberg New Energy Finance projects that the cumulative deployment capacity for the energy storage market will grow from 6 GWh in 2015 to 29 GWh in 2020 and 81 GWh in 2024, a 1,250 percent increase over the ten-year period.[49]

Energy density for size-efficient batteries is extremely important for electric vehicle development, while cost and storage capacity are more important for grid storage batteries.

The lithium-ion battery, the current standard for both electric vehicles and consumer electronics, has made significant gains in recent years, but scientists are also exploring other technologies. We may see battery technologies branch between those that are most applicable to vehicles (higher energy density) and those better suited for grid storage (lower cost per capacity). For example, chemists at the University of Waterloo have developed zinc-ion batteries that are long-lasting, safe, and cost half the price of current lithium-ion batteries.[50] Zinc-ion batteries tend to be large and have lower energy density than lithium-ion batteries, but they could have potential grid storage applications due to their cost and safety. Lithium-air, lithium-sodium, lithium-metal, and solid-state lithium batteries are being explored for potential next-generation applications, as are magnesium, aluminum-air, and sodium-ion batteries and graphene supercapacitors.

Regardless of which core technology emerges, batteries are central to the widespread adoption of renewable power generation systems. As solar and wind technologies have already reached the point of maturity, battery technology is our primary focus to understand the directionality and timing toward the emergence of the power catalyst.

BUSINESS MODELS FOR POWER DISTRIBUTION

The final element of change needed to enable a system-wide shift toward the increasing adoption of renewable energy technology is not a technology issue at all. Instead, it deals with the regulatory environment and business models surrounding the way power is bought and sold.

The current economic model for power in the United States is relatively simple. Utility companies sell power and customers buy power. The utility companies are heavily regulated and given monopolies in most parts of the United States, in exchange for which they make most of the investments in power distribution infrastructure. They buy power via long-term purchasing agreements from other companies that operate power plants.

There are two reasons why this model will need to change significantly in order to allow for renewables. The first is that there is no place in the current model to pay energy storage providers, which, as we have discussed, is essential to mitigate power leveling issues when more power is demanded at a specific time than what is produced. The second issue is that in the renewable energy environment, the delineation between buyers and sellers of power becomes blurred. With the emergence of distributed solar, for example, we could envision many entities that both buy and sell power at different times, complicating the system significantly.

Consider the large retail store that installs PV panels on their roof and covered parking lots. During peak sunlight, they may generate more power than they need, at which point they would either store it or sell it back into the grid based on price and the capacity of the storage systems that they may (or may not) have. At night, this same facility would buy power from the grid. We anticipate an environment where tens or hundreds of thousands of entities are buying and selling power in an energy marketplace. Both the physical infrastructure and the economic model will need to shift to accommodate this new reality. Because this is a highly regulated area, changing the economic model requires changes in regulation. The byzantine nature of some aspects of the American regulatory system could unfortunately end up being one of the more significant challenges delaying the widespread adoption of renewables.

CHANGING GLOBAL TRADE

Now that we have examined the trends enabling a power catalyst, we can consider the global effects of increasing renewable energy as a percentage of global energy consumption. As we mentioned previously, this will not constitute a wholesale shift—fossil fuels will not stop being used entirely for centuries in any reasonable long-term energy forecast. However, even reductions to single or low double-digits will have significant global impacts.

Oil price is extremely sensitive to the global dynamics of supply and demand. Consider the example of 2014-2016. Oil was around $105/barrel in 2014, peaking at $109/barrel in June. In 2014, oil prices collapsed to $50/barrel in January and bottomed out at $29 in January 2016. The driver of this collapse was an increase in global oil production, driven in large part by American technological innovation in unconventional (horizontal) drilling. All told, global supply likely rose by around one to three million barrels per day between 2013-2014. Specifically, in North America, production rose by five million barrels per day between 2010-2015—38 percent faster than growth in global demand.[51]

In an environment where the total crude oil production was just under eighty million barrels per day, this may seem insignificant, but it caused oil markets to shift from a supply-constrained to a demand-constrained environment. In this environment, a 3 percent change in supply created an asymmetric 60 percent change in price. We highlight this shift to emphasize the outsized impact that even a marginal decrease in oil demand resulting from the increased use of renewables can have. Renewables are going to become more important not because of specific policy decisions or environmental considerations, but because the economic calculus behind energy decisions is shifting in favor of renewables.

Another area of global impact centers on shipping and global trade. In the current global energy system, some places have oil and gas and others do not. These resources are extracted from the ground and then shipped via large tankers to the areas where they are refined and consumed.

As renewables—combined with effective grid storage technology—allow for the localization of power generation and consumption, it stands to reason that fewer energy resources will need to be shipped.

The United Nations reported that at least 44 percent of international seaborne trade in 2014 consisted of natural resources. The specific breakdown was 17 percent was crude oil, 9 percent petroleum products, 12 percent coal, and 6 percent gas and chemicals. As nearly half of everything that is shipped around the world is some form of a carbon-based energy product, it stands to reason that any reduction to demand for these resources will significantly impact global trade and its associated industries.[52]

A final consideration around oil price and global energy dynamics is centered on how countries specifically view the value of their in-ground oil and gas assets. In general, countries have operated on a scarcity model, working under the assumption that the price of oil will rise over time as less oil is available, and therefore that oil in ground is worth more than oil extracted now. This has led to the moderated production posture by the Organization of Petroleum Exporting Countries (OPEC), which controls— or tries to control—its members' production levels. Many OPEC nations could produce more oil than they currently do if they wanted to. Doing so would require investment and would negatively impact price as well as the pressures and longevity of their oil fields, but it is possible.

As renewable energy technologies evolve and their impact on oil price becomes more apparent, entities will begin to entertain the idea that this might not be the case. This is an interesting point to consider—what behavior will nations take if they decide that their in-ground assets are worth more now than they will be in the future? Will they increase production even though it would depress prices?

We do not presume to understand exactly how this situation will evolve, but there truly are a number of interesting second and third order effects resulting from a major shift in the global energy business. Recall the global economic and geopolitical significance of the shift from coal to oil; it is not unimaginable that the next transition will have similar effects.

MODULARITY AND SCALABILITY

Another broad impact to consider for renewable power generation is that it allows a degree of modularity and scalability that is not possible with many traditional power generation systems. The variance in cost per unit of energy generated between a large plant and a small plant is far less in renewables than it is in gas, coal, or nuclear plants.

To use the most extreme example, the cost of a nuclear power plant is in the billions, regardless of whether the output is large or small. You cannot build a small nuclear power plant cheaply and then add to its capacity and the population it supports grows. You have to build a large, expensive plant that may have more capacity than you need so that you can grow into it. Once you reach that capacity, you have to build another large, expensive plant. The scale is different for coal and natural gas power plants, but the basic economic calculus is the same.

Power generation plants are typically expensive, so it is most cost-efficient to build large facilities, supporting a large grid of power consumers. The result is that traditional power grids favor centralized, dense environments.

Renewables are different. While there are still economies of scale to be gained by large, concentrated solar plants and wind farms, these technologies allow us to scale up and down as needed, and the financial barriers to entry are much smaller. A village, town, or city could build a solar power plant to fit their needs and the price per unit of power generated would not vary significantly whether they started big or small. If the city grows, they can simply add more PV panels without having to borrow millions or billions to build a new power plant.

Lower-cost power generation and effective grid storage batteries would allow power grids to decentralize while still remaining cost efficient. It becomes economically viable to localize power production, storage, and consumption. In effect, we could disaggregate the grid, creating islands of power that will increase resiliency during a natural disaster or a physical or cyberattack to the grid. Solar power specifically can scale from systems designed to power a house to those designed to power cities. This degree of flexibility is simply not available with fossil fuel-based power generation technologies.

This represents golden opportunities for many countries, especially developing economies that lack the resources for large power plants and the distributions networks required to run power across difficult terrain into rural communities. Just as many countries in Africa skipped landline phones and went straight to cell phones, those same countries could skip large-scale energy plants and move straight to distributed energy projects.

To be certain, there are extensive sunk costs to be considered, especially in developed nations. Renewable power generation systems need to be significantly cheaper in order to justify transitioning away from existing investments, especially those that are still being paid for via long-term financing arrangements. There is no way to flip a switch from a preexisting energy network to change it to renewables, and the more an organization has invested, the longer it will take to transition. Companies and public sector leaders will have to find a way to navigate the financial commitments, which may ultimately be another advantage for developing nations that do not have these sunk costs and switching costs to overcome.

The correlation between prosperity and access to energy is clear: according to the UN-sponsored Human Development Index (HDI), countries with a higher annual per capita energy use have a directly correlated higher HDI, a measure of basic human well-being.[53] Eliminating steep investment hurdles such as multibillion-dollar nuclear power factories and multimillion-dollar coal and gas plants creates new opportunities to facilitate growth and increases in the global standard of living.

The modular nature of renewable energy opens up great potential for developing nations to provide services to their citizens in a financially responsible fashion. These systems will allow the ability to scale from a house to a village to a city by adding capacity in an incremental fashion based on need, which is far better for cash-poor communities than the large up-front investments required for traditional power generation systems.

POWER TECHNOLOGIES AND THE PRIVATE SECTOR

The increasing availability and adoption of renewable

power generation technologies will affect business leaders and investors far beyond the energy sector. To begin with the most obvious, traditional oil and gas exploration companies and the related oilfield services and logistics companies will have to shift substantially. They will need to evaluate the potential for renewables to offset even a small portion of global energy demand, how that will translate into price movements, and what those price movements could mean for their companies. Those organizations are, in some cases, at the forefront of renewable technology innovation, and there are many options available that will allow them to participate in this shift and make investments and divestitures to minimize the impact.

To broaden the focus, there are a number of goods and services tied to the price of energy, which is a consideration for the operating costs of all different types of companies. Companies that procure and pay for energy in one way may now have options to do this in new ways in the near future, which could affect operating costs and budgets. Additionally, as the economics of the energy business shift, so will the price and relative value of these different types of assets.

Having very broadly covered the more obvious economic impacts in the energy and related sectors, we would like to focus on what is perhaps a less obvious impact. What does it mean when all of a business's land and facilities can be considered productive assets in and of themselves? This will certainly be more true in some parts of the world than others, but we can imagine an environment where PV panels and even wind turbines are placed on top of all of our buildings, parking lots, roads, freeways, distribution centers, and even trucking fleets.

As these technologies advance, leaders will have increasing options to integrate them into existing business assets. The world's first solar-powered road was opened in France in 2016. Researchers from the Royal Melbourne Institute of Technology developed a solar-powered paint in 2017, which generates hydrogen fuel from moist air and sunlight.[54] This is certain to be the beginning of these types of integrations.

What does it mean to the real estate industry if every single piece of real estate, occupied or unoccupied, sold or on the market, is a money-making asset? If each property hosts a sheet of solar cells, then even vacant properties can generate revenue. As a catalyst, this shift will require new types of thinking about what are and are not productive assets, and how to maximize an organization's assets in the most productive fashion. Some companies will undoubtedly opt to do nothing, which will probably not doom those organizations but could certainly result in missed opportunities that others will seize.

POWER TECHNOLOGIES AND THE PUBLIC SECTOR

Public sector leaders need to understand this shift and how their countries and organizations fit into the energy and power generation landscape. Those who are heavily reliant on the extraction of fossil fuel should think about their diversification and risk mitigation options. These resources are not limited to a few select regions. Sun and wind are available in most parts of the world, and all nations will have the opportunity to participate in this transition.

Those responsible to regulate and oversee regulatory bodies in this space should proactively evaluate the business environment that they have created. The United States will miss a huge opportunity if we reach the point where renewable technologies at scale are mature but left unused because of outdated regulations and political pressure from entrenched stakeholders.

Public sector leaders can also think about the investments required to facilitate and enable these technologies. While subsidies have had a role in encouraging adoption, we are nearing or are at the point where subsidy programs are no longer required and, in some cases, are becoming counterproductive. Public sector investors should focus their efforts on implementation technologies, as opposed to programs to facilitate adoption, because adoption will happen on its own as a result of market pressures.

Another key consideration for public sector leaders will be the national and international security impacts. Back in 2004, access to electricity was a difference-maker in the war in Iraq. Saddam Hussein kept a stranglehold on power prior to the US invasion in 2003, hoarding the power created by out-of-date, underserviced, overused power plants that he shared only with his political allies. As a result, the wealthy Sunnis lived with almost constant power, while the Shia communities were forced to live with hours of brownouts and blackouts each day, especially during the worst heat of the day. After his overthrow by coalition forces, the large middle class in Iraq began shipping in air conditioners, refrigerators, microwave ovens, TVs, and satellite dishes, significantly increasing the aggregate demand for power. The entire country struggled to keep pace with the sudden uptick in demand for power, forcing the Sunnis to share an already meager supply, intensifying an already strained relationship.

The Sunnis turned their new frustration toward the Americans. In their eyes, the Americans had promised improvement, but the loss of political favoritism within the now more heavily Shia-influenced Iraqi government had actually made things worse. The Shia were not content with their new access to electricity either, because it still meant brownouts and blackouts, and confidence in the Americans was further diminished. Both populations were disenfranchised, in part as a result of electricity issues. Violent extremist organizations in Iraq, such as Al-Qaeda, took advantage of the restlessness and frustration.

Saddam Hussein was aware of the electrical grid's shortcomings and how important it was to mask them. When the furnaces and generators would go down in Baghdad, he would have the workers start fires underneath the smokestacks in order to hide the shortage. A lack of power, he understood, was a sign of weakness. From this history, we grasp the importance of access to energy. In addition to the positive effect of the availability of power on human development, power can be a political tool, and we will likely see that more energy options benefit people at the expense of despots.

Just as energy security is closely correlated with national security, there is also a geopolitical component to renewables. Countries that rely on imports to satisfy an internal energy demand are fundamentally exposed, and to some degree reliant, on energy exporters. Energy exporters—most notably Russia—use price-and-supply favoritism as political tools to extract political concessions. There are countries whose entire foreign policy rests on these mechanisms. Conversely, the countries exposed to those machinations from their neighbors would significantly benefit from access to any degree of increased control over energy supply.

SOLUTIONS

This catalyst represents an exciting suite of developments, but as with each of these transformations, it brings risks along with opportunities. Leaders who are thoughtful and proactive about this shift will enable their organizations to access incredible new opportunities. Conversely, those who are reactive and focused on protecting old business and political models will see only the threats. Getting ahead of this catalyst requires us to reconsider public and private sector assets, rework our economic and regulatory systems, and think about redefining power as a service more than just a transactional, consumable resource.

Countries that derive a large part of their revenue from hydrocarbon-based extractive industries will face an existential challenge. Without much diversity in the economy outside of hydrocarbons, they will need to make a major shift going forward, and their success or failure will affect the global geopolitical environment. The United Arab Emirates has already made some of these moves, diversifying into financial and tourism-driven industries to augment their oil- and gas-based economy. Dubai and Abu Dhabi have become global centers of wealth thanks to these efforts. Saudi Arabia's planned IPO of the state-owned oil company (and largest company in the world) Saudi Aramco should also be viewed in this context.

These advances converge with other global catalysts that

affect where people live—from dispersed suburban and rural communities to more centralized towns and cities. When we lived on farms and rural areas before the invention of electricity, power was generated on-site. Waterfalls powered mills, driving local industry with local energy. The recent iteration of nuclear, gas, and coal power has untethered communities from energy production, but the time may be coming where we will be drawn back toward local, sustainable power solutions, with significant impacts on how and where we live.

Public sector leaders must understand and proactively lead their organizations and constituents through this transition. There is an incredible opportunity here for cities and countries of all sizes and levels of development, but there are also risks for those who fail to appreciate the breadth and significance of this emerging catalyst.

DEMOGRAPHICS

The nature and value of work is changing as a result of converging demographic and technological forces. Birth rates in most developed nations have been declining for decades, and below-replacement-level birth rates will soon be reflected in those countries' productivity and financial stability. Both public-sector entities and private-sector leadership will need to adjust to account for shifts in labor availability and consumer preferences.

LIKELIHOOD OF OCCURRENCE

IMPACT ON INDUSTRY

IMPACT ON THE PUBLIC SECTOR

AVAILABILITY OF SOLUTIONS

Just as we are focused on the broad effects of changes to how and where people live, food production technologies, and how they power their lives, changes to demographics—the fundamental characteristics of a people group—are crucial.

We are currently experiencing the maturation of a demographics revolution that has been in the works for the past fifty years. For the first time in human history, populations in many first world countries are aging—and in many cases, shrinking—on a sustained basis. This has drastic implications for both industry and public sector leaders and hits directly at the heart of geopolitics and national competitiveness.

Demographics is a catalyst that is driving a fundamental restructuring of economic and social activity, which manifests as changes to buying and consumption patterns, social support structures, and living and transportation requirements.

TRENDS

There has never been a time in history, outside of perhaps the Black Death in the fourteenth century and a handful of other event-driven tragedies, when the human population has endured a sustained decline, even on a localized basis. Yet this is what we see happening now in many parts of the world. This is a new phenomenon in human history, and many of the economic and structures that were built using assumptions of normal, growing demographics will need to be reconsidered.

There are currently 7.4 billion people inhabiting this

earth, but the forward-looking trends are dramatically different than what was expected in the 1960s. The total world population is growing at a rate of 1.1 percent, which represents around half the rate of the late 1960s. That is interesting, to be sure, but more significant is the divergence in demographic trajectories between developed and developing nations. While many developing nations are still growing at a normal, rapid pace, developed nations in general began having fewer children in the second half of the twentieth century. Specifically, they began to have fewer children than would be needed to keep the population flat, where births equal deaths. We are at least two generations into this trend, which is now manifesting in an imbalance between workers and retirees in more developed countries, specifically in Asia and Europe. Demographic regression is a slippery slope that is incredibly difficult to change, as we will see.

FERTILITY RATES BY DEVELOPMENT AND INCOME
SIGNIFICANT DIVERGENCE IN POPULATION GROWTH RATES

Fertility Rate by Development Level

Regional Development Level	Fertility Rate*
More Developed Regions	1.67
Less Developed Regions	2.65
Least Developed Countries	4.27
World Average	2.51

Fertility Rate by Income Level

Country Income Level	Fertility Rate*
High-Income Countries	1.75
Middle-Income Countries	2.42
Low-Income Countries	4.89
World Average	2.51

*2010-2015 fertility rates, which represent the average number of births per women

Source: United Nations, Department of Economic and Social Affairs, Population Division (2015). World Population Prospects: The 2015 Revision, DVD Edition.

The United Nations estimates that forty-eight countries will decline in population between 2015–2050.[55] This is somewhat optimistic, given that eighty-three countries had below-replacement-level fertility rates during 2010–2015. The replacement fertility rate is generally cited as 2.1 children per woman of childbearing age. Europe, as a whole, had a fertility rate of 1.6 from 2010 to 2015, which is optimistically projected to grow slightly to 1.8 by the 2045–2050 period. The fact is, Europe is shrinking. European nations have more deaths than new births. Today, 24 percent of the population of Europe is over the age of sixty, the largest ratio of any region in the world.

To cite the obvious, lower birth rates over time result in fewer people. There are a number of examples of this that provide interesting math to consider. During the 2010–2015 period, twenty-five countries had fertility rates below 1.5 children per woman, which is significantly below the replacement rate. The Austrian think tank IIASA published a paper in 2008 that extrapolated that if the global fertility rate shrank to 1.5—near the rate Europe is at now—the world's population would shrink by half in 2200 and fall to one billion by 2300.[56] This is not a scenario that experts consider to be likely, but it is striking nonetheless.

This trend also changes the ratio of young people to old people and workers to retirees, and an increase in the average age of a nation. Demographics impact national productivity and GDP growth, which make shifts extremely meaningful for the affected countries, as well as their trade partners and the companies that operate in those markets. It is important we not dismiss demographic decline as an interesting trend that will lead to more space for everyone left or a boon to sustainability efforts. Societies and the tax bases on which they operate are built on assumptions of certain ratios of contributors versus consumers. Companies also make assumptions about customers and their preferences. As these assumptions change, the structures and strategies that are built on those assumptions must also shift.

Population pyramids are visual representations of the distribution of age groups in a group of people. Growing populations look like a pyramid, as we see in Nigeria. Several things happen in a country, such as Spain, with a flat or inverted population pyramid. The first is that as the median age shifts, so do the median public services required, consumer products preferred, types of housing and transportation needed, and so forth. The second is that the distribution of producers versus consumers in the economy shifts. In growing demographic pools, there are many workers (young) supporting few retirees (old). In flat or shrinking demographic pools, you have fewer workers supporting more retirees. This significantly affects the labor available for companies and public institutions, as well as aggregate state- and national-level productivity (and competitiveness). It also upsets or inverts the economic models that social support networks are built on.

DEMOGRAPHIC POPULATION PYRAMIDS
EXAMPLES OF GROWING AND SHRINKING DEMOGRAPHIC PROFILES

Nigeria: A Positive (Growing) Demographic

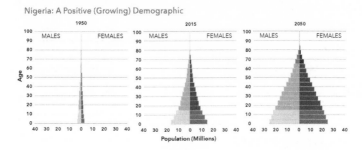

Spain: A Negative (Shrinking) Demographic

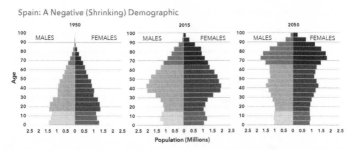

Source: Demographic Profiles, United Nations, Department of Economic and Social Affairs, Population Division, accessed January 22, 2018, https://esa.un.org/unpd/wpp/Graphs/DemographicProfiles/.

Economic productivity is not purely a function of labor; it includes efficiency, technology, and capital as well. Still, as a rule, fewer workers generally results in reduced productivity. Countries with shrinking labor pools should anticipate lower growth rates. Because economic strength measured by GDP growth is viewed as an element of national competitiveness, shrinking labor pools have a detrimental effect on national competitiveness.

A reduction in workers also has a negative impact on the tax base as fewer workers contribute less tax revenue. This issue is specifically dangerous when the number of retirees supported by tax revenues remains flat or increases while the number of workers decreases. The United Nations uses a metric called the potential support ratio (PSR), which is the ratio of people aged twenty to sixty-four, to those aged sixty-five and older. In 1950, when the global median age was twenty-three, the global PSR was around 12. In 2015, the global median age increased to around thirty, and the PSR reduced to 8. It is anticipated to be around 4 in 2050.

DEMOGRAPHICS AND LABOR
RATIO OF WORKERS AGE 20-64 TO RETIREES AGE 65+

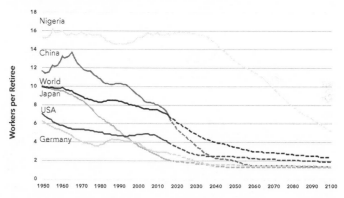

Source: World Population Prospects: The 2015 Revision, DVD Edition, United Nations, Department of Economic and Social Affairs, Population Division, 2015.

While we are less focused on why this trend is happening than what it means for business and public sector leaders, we see several reasons for the demographic decline in the first world. An obvious root cause is that in agrarian and less developed societies, children are an economic benefit to the family, providing more workers to support the household. The world has changed, though. Since the Industrial Revolution and certainly post digital revolution, children, from a purely economic standpoint, have become more of a cost than benefit. The trend toward secularism in the developed world is also a factor, as families who claim a religious affiliation have more children than those who do not (1.7 for unaffiliated versus 2.4 for Hindus, 2.7 for Christians, and 3.1 for Muslims worldwide between 2010–2015).[57] Also impactful is the increasing participation of women in the workforce, the delayed average age of marriage, increasing availability and effectiveness of contraceptives, and perhaps less quantifiable forces such as the cultural and psychological aftereffects of the world wars of the twentieth century.

Regardless of the root cause, this shift is significant and has been building for some time. Leaders in all developed countries, even the United States—which has a healthier demographic profile than Europe and Asia but still faces challenges—must reflect on what this shift means for their organizations. The demographic pressures in the United States are offset to some extent by immigration, but American women are also having fewer children. Between 1976 and 2014, the share of American families with zero to two children increased from 42 percent to 68 percent, while the share of families with three-plus children decreased from 59 percent to 32 percent, based on a sample of American women aged forty to forty-four by the number of children born.

AMERICAN FAMILY SIZE TRENDS
SIGNIFICANT DECLINE IN 3+ CHILDREN FAMILIES BETWEEN 1976 AND 2014

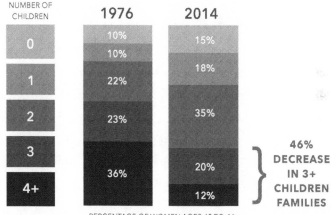

PERCENTAGE OF WOMEN AGES 40 TO 44

Source: George Gao, "Americans' Ideal Family Size Is Smaller Than It Used to Be," Pew Research Center, May 8, 2015, http://www.pewresearch.org/fact-tank/2015/05/08/ideal-size-of-the-american-family/.

The social systems, business models, and supporting infrastructure that were created when the average family had four children need to be reevaluated in the context of older people and smaller families. Even though the United States has a relatively favorable demographic profile when compared to other developed nations, this is a significant issue in other areas of the world, and the data is staggering.

Every new generation of Spaniards is projected to be 40 percent smaller than the previous one.[58] The Portuguese are facing the loss of as much as one-third of their population over the next forty years. Italians over the age of sixty-five are projected to grow from 2.7 percent of the population in 2014 to 18.8 percent in 2050.

DEMOGRAPHICS AND IMMIGRATION

Looking globally, we see that demographic decline is not a universal phenomenon. Many countries are growing, some quite rapidly, which is a new facet in the divide between developing and developed countries. Most of the global population increase is anticipated to come from a relatively short list of countries, many of which are in Africa. Around half of the total global population increase is projected to come from just nine countries: India, Nigeria, Pakistan, Democratic Republic of the Congo, Ethiopia, United Republic of Tanzania, the United States, Indonesia, and Uganda, listed in order of the size of their contribution to the total population growth.

The downward trend in birth rate, in other words, does not affect all regions equally, and immigration rates and policies governing the movement of people from countries gaining in population is an important element to consider going forward. This is specifically important for the United States, which has historically been far better at assimilating immigrants into our workforce and economy than European and Asian nations, for a number of cultural and political reasons. The United States has the world's largest immigrant population, with approximately one in five immigrants worldwide coming to the United States.[59]

Immigration has been an important driver of American growth throughout the nation's history. The United States grew from 193 million people in 1965 to 324 million people in 2015. According to data compiled by the Pew Research Center, 55 percent of American growth over that fifty-year period was due to immigration (72 million of the 131 million-person increase). The contribution of immigrants to total American population gain is even more significant on a forward-looking basis. From 2015 to 2065, the United States is expected to grow from 324 to 441 million people. This would represent a net increase of 117 million people in the next fifty years, similar to the 131 million-person increase over the prior fifty years. What is different going forward is that 88 percent of this growth is projected to result from immigration, or 103 million of the 117 million increase.[60] Also notable is that Asians are projected to surpass Hispanics as the largest immigrant group to the United States over the next fifty years.

Without immigration, the United States population is estimated to remain essentially flat over the next fifty years, from 324 million to 328 million people, with an important worsening of the demographic profile in terms of the ratio between American workers and retirees. This is extremely important. There are myriad considerations that must be carefully measured when it comes to immigration, and the politics surrounding the topic can be volatile, but the fact that immigration plays a fundamental role in American demographic strength is important to understand.

European countries have struggled to open up immigration policies in response to the demand for workers that their populations simply cannot meet. Germany, Europe's strongest economic power, has tried to lead the charge on this front with its pro-immigration and refugee policies, as their economic growth requires an influx of skilled workers to fill approximately 120,000 job positions in science, technology, and engineering, but these policies have been politically difficult to implement. According to the Cologne Institute for Economic Research, that gap may widen to a deficit of one million workers by 2020.[61]

DEMOGRAPHICS AND ROBOTICS

As aging workers retire, there are fewer workers to support manufacturing requirements. Businesses that operate factories can increase wages to attract workers up to a point, but eventually difficult decisions must be made about shrinking facilities, relocating, or retooling. At some point, the shortage of workers becomes a drag on the economy, especially as the bulge of retirees who require public benefits grows beyond the capacity of available workers to support them. The point at which this actually affects an economy differs on a country-by-country basis. In some countries, this is a critical issue now; in others, it will emerge slowly in upcoming years.

Countries have two primary options to fill this gap: get more workers or use technology to offset the number of workers required. Many countries will opt for a holistic approach, incorporating both selective immigration and technology investments. Others will skew toward one side or the other, based on their cultural or geographic predispositions; this is a challenging issue and does not involve just economics but also cultural, political, and social considerations. Focusing on technological solutions, demographics and the resulting market pressures will incentivize the integration of robotics and automation in the workforce as labor shortages increase costs and reduce capacity.

Not all jobs can be replaced or enhanced by robotics and automation, but many can, and demographic decline and labor shortage issues will incentivize adoption of robotics. In the near term—say, the next five years—the majority of automation will continue to occur in the manufacturing sector. Industrial automation tools are capital-intensive, complex systems that we increasingly see in car manufacturing plants and large industrial facilities. Foxconn Technology Group, a major supplier to Apple and Samsung, is an example of this phenomenon. Foxconn reported replacing sixty thousand workers with robots in May 2016 and has the stated goal of having robots constitute 30 percent of its 1.3 million-person workforce by 2020.[62]

We anticipate many growing areas of robotics applications in the near term, some of which we are seeing now. Handling and warehouse operations—including palletizing, metal machining, and plastic molding—as well as manufacturing operations—including assembly, disassembly, and spot and arc welding—are or will move toward robotics. We will also see an increase in industrial, agricultural, and surveying drones, as well as driverless trains, buses, and mining vehicles.

In the longer term, we anticipate a more pervasive integration of robotics into the consumer, service, health-care, and other sectors. Robots even have the potential to expand into the "creative" potential, as evidenced by the Associated Press's automated reporting platform Wordsmith,[63] which has covered sports, finance, and other topics.

Other types of robotics that we anticipate include transportation—including autonomous public and private vehicles—artificial assistants and in-home elderly support and childcare, education—especially in programs to help children with special needs—and more expansive medical procedures and operations. Home service robots are becoming increasingly important to support in-house care needs for the elderly in Japan, which has among the worst demographics in the world.

While automation certainly represents a disruption and challenge, it is important to note that labor patterns have never been fixed. Developed economies in particular constantly deal with transitions and displacement and have demonstrated resiliency, which we will discuss in further detail when we address technology as a catalyst.

DEMOGRAPHICS' IMPACT ON THE PRIVATE SECTOR

Demographics touch every area of the economy. In essence, demographics represent a reflection of the mix and dynamics of people, and people are the economy. Some economic sectors are impacted more directly than others, but demographics matter to hiring, training, marketing, selling, building, governing, teaching, policing, voting, transporting, investing, insuring, and virtually every other activity one can think of. As the average and median age increases, there is a corresponding shift to aggregate consumer preferences. After all, one's age and family requirements heavily influence what one buys—

from food to furniture and fashion. This is meaningful both from a style and base requirements perspective, and companies will be forced to adapt their products and services to meet the needs of the "new" consumer. This knowledge should drive product strategy and dictate how brands position themselves going forward.

Japan can be viewed as a leading indicator for this shift, as the Japanese demographic decline is extremely advanced. The fertility rate in Japan is 1.2 children per woman of childbearing age, among the lowest in the world. This has had major consequences for the country's economy. A striking example is projections in Japan that adult diapers will outsell baby diapers by 2020.[64] This is a significant shift from the prior norm. While this is a single, albeit memorable, example, these types of shifts are occurring throughout all categories of consumer products.

Age and family composition also change living preferences, impacting the size of houses and the distribution between single-family home versus apartment living, as well as urban versus suburban living. This shift will take time to manifest into changes in demand and asset prices but will ultimately be important for both homebuilders and real estate investors as they think about strategy in upcoming years. A neighborhood built in anticipation of housing retirees will need different types of floor plans and amenities than one made for families with young children.

Demographics also affect transportation requirements and automobile purchasing preferences in a similar fashion to our discussion on urban versus rural living. Just as where you live determines your transportation needs, how you live also affects these needs. This will be reflected both in vehicle purchase considerations, such as the ratio of family-oriented cars to those oriented to retirees, as well as the demand for senior-friendly public transportation and third-party transportation-as-a-service providers.

These brief examples are the tip of the iceberg. Every industry and business that deals with people at scale will feel the effect of this demographics shift in some fashion. The speed and scope of change varies according to the demographic profile of each country and region, but the impact will be global in nature. Companies that operate from countries with favorable demographics, such as the United States, still need to understand the trend as they operate in the context of a global marketplace that is rapidly changing.

DEMOGRAPHICS AND THE PUBLIC SECTOR

There are a number of different ways in which demographics interact with public sector leadership and responsibilities. The first and most obvious area of interaction is with government services. The services that governments provide to their constituents are based on needs, which vary according age and lifestyle. Older people need different programs than children. The ratio and breakdown of funding required for child and retiree programs will shift as the age distribution shifts, but equally important is the way that services are consumed is also predicated in part by age, which drives how they must be delivered. Budgets and policies must be revisited and evolved to ensure that they meet the needs of constituents as they are today, as opposed to as they were in the past.

The starkest and most potentially worrisome element of demographic decline is the negative impact it has on the tax base and how that is reflected in funding for retirement programs. All countries have built their retirement and social support programs on an anticipated ratio of contributors into the system and withdrawers from the system. The American Social Security system, for example, is constructed so that multiple workers make contributions for each retiree who makes withdrawals. This is done more or less directly in different types of country-level retirement programs, but all such programs are built on this math.

These systems encounter a significant challenge when the ratio of contributors and withdrawers shifts. In an environment with the converging forces of declining demographics and more capable medical technology, there will be fewer workers and more retirees who live longer in retirement. Fewer contributors and more withdrawers is a problem at the fundamental mathematical level—either the contributions have to increase, the withdrawals have to decrease, or cuts have to be made elsewhere in order for these systems to be sustainable.

If the demographic decline continues as projected, countries will have to completely rework their retirement age and social support policies for retirees, which will not be an easy feat. Policies that were put in place globally during a time when you had seven workers per retiree, as the United States did in 1950, mathematically will not work in an environment when you have four workers per retiree, as the United States did in 2015, or 2.4 workers per retiree as it is projected to have in 2050.[65]

Policy needs to catch up to new realities created by demographics in a number of areas. Another example is seen in the communities of single-family residences where schools were built to handle the children of suburban neighborhoods. As these children graduate college, the homes are too expensive for new families and they are choosing to not return to the suburbs, instead moving to urban areas. Meanwhile, the parents have stayed, meaning there are large schools and similar facilities with no children in them. Yet the schools that were built for previous populations remain, reflecting an inefficient allocation of resources that comes at an opportunity cost for other types of services and programs.

SOLUTIONS

Countries that face negative demographics have several options available to them. They can allow their economies to shrink, attract new workers via immigration, or invest in robotics to try to increase per-worker productivity. In this light, it is illustrative to return to the example of Japan, which has both a negative demographic trajectory and a cultural and policy environment that is prohibitive to immigration.

In an attempt to offset demographic decline, Japan has invested heavily in robotics in an effort to automate many mid-level jobs, making it the leader in the field. With few options left, robotics stands to solve a number of the country's demographics issues. The potential of in-house robots could go as far as to meet the growing need of eldercare in the country. As a benefit of this research, Japanese companies are now exporting robotics technologies internationally, and their expertise in robotics is so pervasive that it has become a national asset.

The aging demographic profile of the developed world changes the foundation on which businesses and governments build strategy. As the foundation changes, those institutions must evaluate for themselves whether or not their core assumptions remain valid, then determine whether (and how) they must adjust in order to remain competitive.

CITIES

Where and how people live drives what they buy, how they vote, and what services they need; huge shifts to these choices are coming as a result of urbanization, the transportation revolution, and the emergence of technology-enabled infrastructure. Cities are being transformed on a scale not seen since the industrial revolution. The impact will reach far beyond city planners and developers; the emerging high-tech urban world will affect all businesses, investors, and social institutions that engage with people at scale.

LIKELIHOOD OF OCCURRENCE

IMPACT ON INDUSTRY

IMPACT ON THE PUBLIC SECTOR

AVAILABILITY OF SOLUTIONS

A number of both technological and social factors are converging to change some of the key elements of cities. Regardless of whether we refer to this as the "smart cities" revolution or merely a technology-enabled transformation, the fact is that cities are changing as a result of several different pressures—urbanization, technology-enabled infrastructure, the mobility revolution, and sustainability pressures resulting from density. Because cities with more than 150,000 inhabitants produce around 85 percent of GDP in the United States, 78 percent in China, and 68 percent in Europe, any transformation has the potential for significant and broad impact.[66]

There are four key elements of convergence. The first element—which has been happening for some time but, in our experience, is not broadly acknowledged—is that more people are moving to cities than ever before, shifting the balance of urban versus rural dwellers, and creating cities that are larger than previously.

Second, we now have the possibility to build technology-enabled infrastructure, with embedded sensors and other data collection and projection capabilities that have never before existed. This is specifically important in the United States, as we are reaching the generational replacement cycle for critical infrastructure all over the country. New infrastructure will have to be built across the country, and the new capabilities and data generation opportunities enabled by these systems will change the way we think of cities.

Third, the revolution in mobility and transportation is maturing, both in terms of the business model shift toward shared ownership and the autonomous vehicle and electric vehicle technologies that are coming online. Fourth, sustainability issues are being exacerbated by scale and density of cities around the world. Similar to technology-enabled infrastructure, new innovations are coming online that will allow for new tools to try and mitigate these sustainability problems.

The convergence of these factors leads us to anticipate a transformation in the shape of cities and the way people, governments, and businesses interact within cities. Where and how people live determines how they work, the products they buy, and the services they need. This transformation holds importance far beyond the urban planning and construction communities. Incremental step-function changes have occurred since the last major transformation to cities resulting from the Industrial Revolution. Now the unprecedented movement of the global population, the new types of infrastructure, and the emergence of new technologies place us in the early stages of a new cycle for cities.

TRENDS

As with any catalyst, we must look closely at the underlying data to help understand the directionality and timing of emerging changes. In terms of smart cities, we can track four major areas of transformation: urbanization, infrastructure, sustainability, and urban mobility.

URBANIZATION AND THE MASS MOVEMENT OF PEOPLE TO CITIES

The data surrounding global migration to large cities is eye-opening. The United Nations in 2009 and the International Organization for Migration in 2015 both estimated that around three million people move to cities every week. Approximately 54 percent of people worldwide now live in cities, up from 30 percent in 1950. Sources estimate this number will grow to two-thirds of the world's population in the next fifteen to thirty years. More than half of urban dwellers live in the 1,022 cities with more than 500,000 inhabitants. Some cities, such as Lagos, Nigeria, have grown in a near-exponential fashion over the last half century, from around 500,000 to nearly seventeen million people.

URBANIZATION
GLOBAL URBAN VS. RURAL POPULATION, 1950-2050

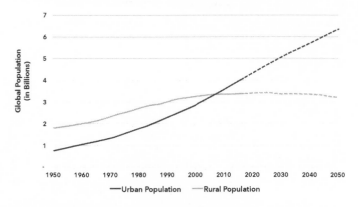

Source: Population Division World Urbanization Prospects 2014, Department of Economic and Social Affairs, United Nations, accessed January 22, 2018, https://esa.un.org/unpd/wup/.

In 1950, there were two megacities, defined as urban areas with a population of more than ten million. Now, the number is twenty-nine, projected to rise as high as fifty-three by 2030. Additionally, there are 468 cities with a population of more than one million, up from eighty-three in 1950. A Yale research group projects that urban land coverage will expand by 463,000 square miles by 2030 to cover just under 10 percent of the planet's land, equivalent to twenty thousand football fields being paved over every day.[67]

This trend is not quite as pronounced in the United States, where much of the initial migration from rural to urban areas has already occurred, but many cities are still experiencing significant growth. Today, 82 percent of North Americans live in urban areas and are increasingly concentrating in midsized and large cities. In 2010, forty-one urban areas in the United States housed more than one million people, up from twelve areas in 1950 and projected by the United Nations to grow to fifty-three by 2030.

Even if the top line population growth of cities in the United States is changing less dramatically than in some other regions, the dynamics within those existing populations are shifting drastically. Certain cities are becoming increasingly synonymous with various sectors of the economy—technology in San Francisco, energy in Houston, and finance in New York—and benefit from network effects that allow them to grow increasingly wealthier, often at the expense of other cities. The concentration of wealth and opportunity creates large population hubs and an emerging divergence between cities that are net gainers and net losers in terms of people, wealth, and economic opportunity.

While we are focused on growth, it is important to note that not all cities in the United States are growing. Growth in the cities that are best positioned to attract talent comes at the expense of those that are not as well positioned. In 2012 and 2013, 92 of the country's 381 metropolitan areas lost population, with cities such as Chicago and Baltimore not only losing population but also significant economic activity.[68] Fewer people and businesses leads to a decrease in tax base, which makes it harder to remain competitive on a number of fronts. These cities have a difficult challenge ahead to mitigate these effects or potentially reverse the trends before they become too difficult to control.

The difficulties around transformation that we have previously discussed apply to cities just as they do to businesses and other public sector institutions. When the environment changes significantly and organizations do not react correctly or quickly enough, they are diminished. Detroit is an excellent example of an urban area that either did not anticipate or did not do enough to react to a significant environmental shift, which resulted in a huge economic and personnel downturn before its current, slow revitalization.

Understanding the driving forces behind a catalyst can help us to understand its trajectory and timing. One obvious driver of urbanization is increased mechanization, automation, and innovation in the agriculture sector. Sophisticated methods and machinery decrease the number of workers required to sustain agricultural production. This is the primary force of much of the migration in developing nations that are in the process of transitioning to more efficient and mechanized agriculture techniques. It will be interesting to see if the integration of drones and autonomous vehicles in the agriculture sector of developed nations creates another round of agricultural efficiency gains and a corresponding wave of urban migration. If that does turn out to be the case, it will affect migration and living patterns in both developing and developed nations.

A second driver of urban migration, which we alluded to previously, is the increasing concentration of industry expertise and wealth into specific cities; this is also driving people toward fewer, larger cities in the United States and other developed economies. Industry centers such as Houston (energy), San Francisco (technology), and New York (finance) are prime examples of areas where

Americans move to build businesses and pursue careers in specific fields. People who have found success in these cities tend to make greater investments in the city, building more companies and sparking an even greater inflow of talent and capital. This is the inverse of a slippery slope that has characterized Detroit and other cities—it is a virtuous cycle.

TECHNOLOGY-ENABLED INFRASTRUCTURE

As cities grow larger, they create new problems and need different types of infrastructure. Among the largest apartment buildings in the world is the Copan Building in São Paulo, which houses more than five thousand people in more than eleven hundred units.[69] The water, HVAC, sanitation, and logistic systems to support this building and others like it are simply different than the systems required to support a less dense population.

New technologies are available to provide for different infrastructure capabilities than ever before. The ability to embed sensors and software-enabled governance systems into physical infrastructure has simply not existed in the past. While the most recent step-function change in infrastructure was focused on materials technology in support of the automobile, the step-function increase in capability that we are currently seeing is driven by software, sensors, and data analytics. These tools and

MEGACITIES

2015 AND 2025 PROJECTIONS OF URBAN AREAS WITH MORE THAN 10 MILLION PEOPLE

*POPULATION
IN MILLIONS

2025
PROJECTION*

2015
PROJECTION*

TOKYO
OSAKA
TIANJIN
SHANGHAI
SHENZHEN
GUANGZHOU
MANILA
BEIJING
WUHAN
CHONGQING
DHAKA
CALCUTTA
BANGKOK
HYDERABAD
CHENNAI
JAKARTA
DELHI
LAHORE
KARACHI
MUMBAI
BANGALORE
MOSCOW
CAIRO
LAGOS
LONDON
PARIS
NEW YORK CITY
SÃO PAULO
BUENOS AIRES
CHICAGO
BOGOTA
LIMA
MEXICO CITY
LOS ANGELES

Source: "Rise of the Megacities—Get the Data," DataBlog, Facts Are Sacred, The Guardian, accessed January 22, 2018,
https://www.theguardian.com/global-development/datablog/2012/oct/04/rise-megacities-get-data#data.

systems that are emerging provide different capabilities than anything we have previously experienced.

New American infrastructure is dearly needed across the country and, regardless of all the political posturing in the United States, will be built as more and more of the critical infrastructure in the United States faces replacement age. It is worth repeating that the infrastructure report card, broken down by aviation, ports, bridges, parks, and so on, graded the United States at a D+ average. American infrastructure is clearly facing the end of its life cycle and must be updated. According to some estimates, the United States requires $3.6 trillion in needed investment by 2020.

What we have is the perfect storm: cities are growing larger than ever before, new types of infrastructure are available, and we are reaching a generational replacement cycle for much of the key infrastructure in the United States. This will look different in different parts of the world, as infrastructure challenges vary from city to city, but most cities face challenges in dealing with pollution, quality of life, congestion, crime, and all the other complications that emerge when massive amounts of people are brought together in close proximity.

Regardless of these differences, each of these factors will result in the changing shape and structure of cities, which represents a massive opportunity and an equally sizable risk for both the public and private sector, because where and how people live determine so much of what they need and use.

SUSTAINABILITY—NEW CHALLENGES AND NEW SOLUTIONS

Sustainability is the third area of change that we see interacting with urbanization, infrastructure, and transportation issues. These forces are all related, and it is less important to understand the delineating borders between each issue than it is to understand the changing system as a whole. We view sustainability issues beyond the paradigm of politics and policy, and we are focused on the very real factors that impact economics, health, and competitiveness at the city level.

Environmental considerations such as air quality, traffic, and disease have become a priority focus for city planners worldwide. There are cities in China, for example, that struggle to attract and retain businesses and businesspeople—representing real economic activity—because the air pollution is out of control. As cities grow larger, these challenges become more difficult to overcome. Megacities of ten, twenty-five, and eventually fifty million people bring specific, practical sustainability requirements to address pollution, trash, and waste that have yet to be solved. The massive movement of people to cities has created significant traffic, air pollution, and waste issues for every single large city around the world.

Similar to our comments about infrastructure, these sustainability challenges are emerging alongside new technology-enabled solutions. A generation of new products and systems is being developed that can mitigate many of these sustainability challenges, just as industries are emerging to address the ecological and health aspects of dense urban living. Some examples are green roof systems to absorb heat and filter air pollutants, rainwater harvesting to support toilet flushing, sanitation systems to reduce water requirements, and localized pollution scrubbers in buildings to allow for healthier conditions in heavily polluted areas. These products and services will range from government investments, to business-focused solutions, to products and services that are marketed and sold to the individual consumer, changing the playing field at all levels.

THE TRANSPORTATION REVOLUTION

The fourth and final element of convergence that we see coming together to change the shape of cities is the transportation revolution. Currently under way, this reflects both a business model and a technology issue. The standard model of transportation in the automobile era is for people to use their privately owned vehicles to move between work, home, entertainment, and whatever else they do with their lives. People have historically owned vehicles, and car manufacturers have been the driving force of the industry.

The rise of transportation-as-a-service providers—most notably Uber and Lyft—is in the process of significantly altering the transportation industry landscape. Vehicle ownership is still the most prominent model but is no longer the only option. Many are beginning to look at transportation as a service (get me there) as opposed to a product (get me a car). This shift was enabled by location-based technologies in the smartphone. The other main technology that will push this industry in the direction of the service model is the continuing development toward autonomous vehicles. It is easy to envision an environment in which those of us who still own cars turn them into revenue-generating assets by putting them into the fleet of vehicles that can be called by others after they drop us off at work.

This is a complex and impactful transformation. The interplay between the transportation revolution and urbanization, infrastructure, and sustainability has significant implications for both businesses and regulators. GPS technology can tell us where people are and where they want to go, but optimizing the timing and orchestration required to get commuters from where they are to where they need to go relies not only on technology but also infrastructure. Part of the problem is that most government regulations were designed for a different time and era. How do we classify a fifteen-passenger van with fifteen people who need to get from point A to point B at a specific time? Is it a ride for hire, taxi, on-time delivery, or bus? Each classification comes with different regulations and laws, most of which are archaic and rarely speak to the needs of the modern commuter.

HOW TRANSFORMING CITIES IMPACT THE PRIVATE SECTOR

Lifestyle choices and consumer preferences drive the strategies that consumer product organizations employ. Product selection, retail footprint, store location, and the style of stores will all be affected as more and more customers move to the city.

In many cases, the go-to-market strategies for companies must be adjusted to reflect the changing nature of their customers. The decline of Main Street America is illustrative of this point. The small businesses that were successful in small towns were devastated by big-box retail when the American population shifted to the suburbs. A similar shift is in play in many countries that are experiencing significant movement of people into cities.

Companies are trying to adjust, but these shifts are difficult to execute at scale. Walmart, to use one example, has recently experimented with smaller-footprint stores in high-density areas. They built these stores under the assumption that city people were not likely to drive out to the suburbs to shop; they were far more likely to shop where they lived. This experiment was revealed as a failure in 2016, when Walmart announced the closure of all 102 of the company's smallest facilities, the Walmart Express stores.[70] This is illustrative of two things: that Walmart understands what is happening and that these shifts are difficult to navigate. Although their initial adjustment was not successful, we applaud Walmart's proactive response and suspect that they will continue to experiment with different models to try to map their business apparatus to their customers as effectively as possible.

The rise of the Internet of Things (IoT) is another interesting factor to consider in the context of urbanization and large cities. IoT is the network of devices, sensors, appliances, and consumer electronics systems connected to each other and to the internet. IHS estimates that there were 17.6 billion connected devices as of 2016. Different groups project that this will increase to around thirty billion devices by 2020.[71] Interconnectedness and proximity of people and devices lead to a number of consumer dynamics that affect a range of industries.

The convergence of more people moving to dense urban

areas, more connected devices per person, and more data used per device is putting a significant strain on current networks, which will only grow over time. Entirely new forms of telecommunications infrastructure will be needed to support the growing demand for bandwidth, which will require significant investment and planning by both the public and private sector.

What does dense urban living mean when businesses sit down to design hardware, software, or even retail spaces to cater to it? A company that builds washing machines, for example, needs to think about the form factor of its products to fit in smaller spaces, how shared or service models could affect the aggregate demand for its products, and how to connect its products into the IoT in a safe and productive fashion. These are clearly different challenges than prior generations of executives in the consumer appliance space faced.

Consider the automobile industry, which as we discussed is already going through a significant transformation. Including the changing shape of transportation patterns and people's travel needs adds another element to this dynamic. Someone using a car in a city has different needs than someone in a rural area and will favor certain characteristics in an automobile. With more people living closer to work, fewer cars will be sold and not as many miles will be driven. Commercial and public transit will become more practical and popular, which will require improved infrastructure and routing to optimize those offerings.

Construction companies building apartment complexes and urban malls will also need to start thinking differently as urban density, changing transportation, new types of infrastructure, and sustainability challenges become bigger issues. Projecting current market demands on a changing future environment is a common but flawed way to approach business planning in this industry. We can envision huge shifts in the construction sector in the coming years, with space and sustainability becoming larger issues. In some cities, for example, shared living spaces for young workers have gained popularity. WeWork, a workspace and residential community throughout the United States, is an excellent example. This $20 billion company was built on the opportunity created by urbanization and emerging technology trends.

Parking is another issue. In the scenario we described previously—where I put my autonomous car in service after it drops me off at work—I do not need to park it. Who will be the commercial developer to build the last large parking garage?

Logistics companies also need to think differently about the transportation network from ports or manufacturing centers, to distribution centers, to retail spaces and the end customer. Related, how does one deliver mail and packages to an apartment building that houses five thousand people in an efficient fashion, all of whom are buying more and more goods on the internet and having them delivered directly? Logistic companies, wholesalers, and retailers will, in many cases, need to transform their organizations to remain competitive. Amazon, for example, is in the midst of building new systems for next-day and same-day delivery and anticipates the exclusive use of drones to achieve faster delivery times across an entire urban landscape. This is a significant shift from traditional air and truck delivery and highlights the need for companies to think about how they want to invest their resources as the fundamental requirements for the how, where, and to whom of basic logistics change.

Every single industry needs to consider how the changing shape of cities impacts their business. Fashion trends change more quickly in cities. City dwellers eat out in restaurants more than suburban families, and they buy groceries more often but in smaller quantities. Different types of HVAC and air-filtration systems work in large facilities versus small, single-family buildings. The dynamics of the insurance business change when fewer people own cars and houses. Power consumption per capita is different for urban versus suburban versus rural living. These are just a few of many changes, and some industries will be impacted more directly than others, but these issues need to be considered for all types of businesses and investors.

HOW TRANSFORMING CITIES IMPACT THE PUBLIC SECTOR

Based on examining the behavior of public institutions in previous times of transformation, we anticipate that some groups will use these technologies to provide enhanced services for their people, while others will fail to keep up with the changes and provide less effective services, to the detriment of their citizens. Although it is not a black-and-white issue, it is worth noting that many governments have struggled in the past to keep pace with technology.

Efficiency of service is what must be considered. The environment has changed; so are the same services needed? Should we drop services that are not needed, add those that the changing environment has created a new requirement for, or both? Should these services be delivered in the same fashion that they always have been? Where can we apply software to make the system more efficient? Who should provide these services? In cities across America, a recent trend finds governments trying to gain efficiency through privatization of services, which leads to many provocative questions about the role of the government. The changing environment requires new types of responses and warrants a revisiting of the types of services that are best provided by the public versus the private sector.

Different tools are also needed in large cities and megacities than in suburban and rural settings. For example, police officers and security personnel require different equipment and training when operating in a vertical environment with narrow streets. Using another example of how the private and public sectors interact, aerospace and defense companies will have to think differently about the platforms they build for their law enforcement and military customers. Drones and intelligence, surveillance, and reconnaissance (ISR) platforms, for example, have become important tools for modern military forces. Counterterrorism operations in a megacity of ten million-plus people mean these instruments will require different types of sensors and software and perhaps even entirely different form factors—think small helicopters that fly at building level versus large airframes that fly at five to ten thousand feet.

As cities grow, efficient transportation becomes more and more important. Most cities are trying to create an environment where public transportation—whether buses, subways, or light rails—can cover a majority of a commuter's trip. Then, there are the smaller ride providers that provide first and last mile solutions to the major public networks. How can these sectors synchronize their systems in order to increase efficiency and make the lives of everyone easier by having the information centralized as part of one ecosystem? Where should the public sector system stop and the private sector system begin? Government leaders and policy makers will have to determine whether they should outsource these solutions and if they are better off as a competitive marketplace as opposed to granting one company a monopoly. Better synchronization will allow people to spend less time in transit and more time contributing to society, whether at work or at home with the family—with a net impact of increasing productivity, to the benefit of everyone.

Cities that ignore the changing landscape will, as a result, lose population to more successful cities, which could start its own cascade of reactions. Decreasing tax bases leads to smaller budgets and less investment, which in turn drives more of the population away. Our challenge is to facilitate the virtuous cycle of success and avoid the slippery slope of missed opportunities.

THE AUSTIN CASE STUDY

Austin, Texas, has been a case study for city growth for some time. For generations, Austin was known primarily as a college town. This view was, for the most part, correct. Austin was essentially a large university with a community built around it, although it carried the added benefit of being the capital of the state, which attracted legislators and other government offices. There was nothing particularly special about Austin until city leadership made a strategic decision to attract specific types of talent to the area. By the 1980s, the city had realized that the boom-to-bust cycle of the local energy industry and the transient university and government communities were not a solid foundation for a city. They created a strategic road map to incentivize technology companies to open in or relocate to Austin.

IBM and National Instruments soon set up shop in Austin and began to attract talented software engineers, technologists, and entrepreneurs to the area, which led to the formation of more technology companies. One of the most well-known and successful examples is Dell. The city cross-pollinated those businesses and professionals with other local talent and events, such as South by Southwest, which began as a music festival and then became a film conference, before finally becoming one of the premier technology events in the world. Within the last five years, Austin has become a place where global investors and government leaders come to meet innovators.

Following this road map did not come without its bumps. In the early 2000s, Austin suffered from the dot-com bubble burst, which provided a valuable lesson about diversification across industries and economic sectors.

The result was an organization called Opportunity Austin, whose goal was to diversify and look for opportunities in manufacturing, medical services, and bioscience—anything they could bring into the city beyond computers and chip technology. Today, Austin is stronger than ever thanks to a self-sustaining, diverse ecosystem led by an entrepreneurial culture that is constantly creating new opportunities, which in turn attracts more talented men and women. But as with all progress, new challenges emerge that must not be ignored. Austin is currently struggling with a growing affordability issue as the cost of living has gone up quickly, especially in housing prices. There is also a gap in socioeconomic opportunity that is one of the widest in the country.[72]

In early May 2017, *Forbes* magazine predicted that the entire region from Austin to San Antonio was going to become the next great US metropolis. Twenty or thirty years ago, such a prediction would have looked fantastical. There is a vibrant cross-sector growth in the city that comes from a local government committed to prioritizing growth and success in the region. The niche skills, talents, and research fostered at the University of Texas, Texas State University, and University of Texas at San Antonio contribute to advancements in computers, cybersecurity, and renewable energy storage and production. The government and military centers in the region invest in these technologies, and the private companies that have been drawn to the region figure out ways to monetize these advancements.

This trend is present in other cities as well. When Indianapolis faced the series of economic pressures commonly known as the Rust Belt alongside Detroit, it took active steps to diversify by investing in entertainment and tourism. An investment in sports and the supporting facilities brought people and resources to the city and allowed them to revitalize the downtown area. Simultaneously, the city established technology and entrepreneurship funds, planting the seeds to become a major hub of innovation, wealth, and people. Detroit faced a larger uphill battle, but its leaders were also less agile and slower to transition away from old models. The most poignant lesson from Austin, Indianapolis, and Detroit is that proactive strategy leads to more productive outcomes than reactive policies. Austin has followed a strategic blueprint for decades to get to its current point of growth and future potential.

SOLUTIONS

This transformation in cities provides tremendous opportunities to bring people, resources, and technology together for the benefit of all sectors of our society and economy. Urbanization provides new opportunities for businesses to excel and support their customers and new opportunities for government to enable their constituents' growth and success. There are no clear right and wrong answers, but it is important to realize that the productivity and innovation gains that can come out of these systems will be self-accelerating. Some cities and countries are going to more effectively enable growth than others—and talent, capital, and innovation will flow to those areas, away from other places. In a world where national borders matter less for business operations, cities effectively become the playing field for national and regional competitiveness.

In cities, we commonly find an overlapping and some-times aligned interests between industry, government, and research institutions. Businesses and innovators pro-vide solutions, but government brings a unique ability to implement these solutions and technologies at scale. The ideal environment for growth is one in which government policy is designed to facilitate alignment between these sectors. Too often, we see an environment that artificially fosters a winner-take-all mentality between important pil-lars of society, which is a flawed and dangerous approach toward policy and governance in a rapidly changing world.

These transformations are happening whether we wish and prepare for them or not. The transformation of cities will change the way large segments of the global popu-lation live and work. Businesses that do not adapt their products, services, and distribution efforts are at risk of being displaced by companies that do. Similarly, public and academic institutions that do not evolve with the environment risk being diminished. As leaders, we must shift our perspectives to match the environment and expose ourselves to new ways of approaching old problems, difficult though that may be.

9

TECHNOLOGY

The accelerating pace of change enabled by computers and software is creating an environment where technology outpaces the adaptability of our business, political, and social institutions. While technology plays a role in all catalysts, machine learning, augmented reality, health, and finance are key areas of emerging transformation that will fundamentally alter the industry dynamics for most companies and public institutions.

LIKELIHOOD OF OCCURRENCE

IMPACT ON INDUSTRY

IMPACT ON THE PUBLIC SECTOR

AVAILABILITY OF SOLUTIONS

Many of the most prominent and fastest-occurring catalysts are a result of technological advances. Innovations such as the printing press, steam and internal combustion engines, electricity, and personal computers have indisputably created new market paradigms and altered the course of history. Technology has also enabled or set the conditions for many of the other catalysts we have discussed. Urbanization and demographics are rooted in changes to agricultural and medical technology, manufacturing is changing as a result of 3D printing technology, and renewable energy technologies are the core of the power catalyst. Technology is not a stand-alone category; it is interwoven through every catalyst in some fashion.

In this section, we will focus on the emerging fields of machine learning, genomics and biotechnology, augmented reality, and blockchain. What follows are short descriptions of the specific areas and technologies that we believe to have the highest potential for transformative, system-wide impacts, followed by a discussion of several of the most broadly important second and third order effects. We have not tried to provide a comprehensive summary of the current state of R&D in each field; rather, our aim is to highlight where we see these technologies going as they mature. Whether or not you believe your field is highly affected by these technological developments, you will want to understand these trends. In some way, they will affect everyone.

All of these categories of technology are enabled by computing power. The exponential gains in processing power over the past five decades has enabled an explosion of creativity, which will continue to accelerate as a result of advanced computing technologies. The 22-core Xeon

Broadwell-E5, released by Intel in 2016, contains 7.2 billion transistors—a far cry from Intel's 4004 processor released in 1971, which contained 2,300 transistors.[73] This amazing increase has enabled a cascade of technological developments.

COMPUTING ENABLES NEW TECHNOLOGIES
MOORE'S LAW AND EXPONENTIAL INCREASES IN COMPUTING POWER

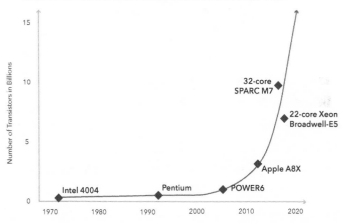

Source: "Transistor Count," Wikipedia, edited December 29, 2017, https://en.wikipedia.org/wiki/Transistor_count.

TRENDS IN MACHINE LEARNING

Until recent years, computers have been generally thought of as command-driven machines. Men and women built them and wrote software that provided a detailed set of instructions or rules that determined *if* a certain thing happened, *then* a certain action would be triggered. Software applications have grown increasingly sophisticated, but they are still a set of commands. As a result, computers have been limited by human speed and imagination, as machines could only perform the instructions that they had been given.

Machine learning and artificial intelligence (AI) are changing this fundamental paradigm of how computers execute instructions and how they interact with humans. Machine learning and AI are two related and, at a practical level, somewhat interchangeable terms. We view them on a spectrum of capability ranging from machines that access data and learn for themselves (machine learning) to the broader concepts of machines that simulate or imitate intelligent behavior (AI). For this discussion, we will focus on machine learning, as that will be the root of most applications that we see in the next few years.

The fundamental change at the core of machine learning is the transition from a human-command-driven engine to a machine-inference engine. An inference engine is software that applies logical rules to a data set to infer new information. This shift is extremely significant, as it results in software that is increasingly capable of developing and refining its own instructions to perform tasks without the limiting factor of a human being needing to provide every instruction.

As machine-learning systems become increasingly capable, we move further away from predictable, strict processes and outcomes. Computer systems can now refine their understanding of the task and the environment based on the information it gathers every time it takes an action. This is an extremely important change from traditional computing. This will enable new types of problem solving and the ability to process more information in new and complex ways, enabling entirely new types of machine capabilities. A related challenge is that software engineers may no longer be able to retroactively map or audit the path an algorithm followed to understand how a system arrived at a certain point. It is less transparent and more complicated.

The latest iteration of software development has been focused on mobile, cloud, and location-based technologies; the next will be based on machine learning. Machine learning is the next evolution of software development. Just as venture capitalist Marc Andreessen noted that "software is eating the world," many technologists have pointed out that "AI is eating software." Machine-learning algorithms will be applied to the majority of our existing software tools to create new experiences and capabilities—ranging from maps and digital assistants to accounting and industrial applications. When computers are able to infer new instructions from both data inputs and prior outcomes to make better decisions, this will have the secondary effect of significantly increasing the value of large sets of data, which we will discuss in further detail.

These developments are in production in many cases, and software engineers are already developing advanced algorithms with machine-learning capabilities that will continue to get more and more complex and capable over time. Those machine-learning capabilities can be integrated into every software platform in use today and will soon impact every software interaction in our daily lives—from health care to finance, from education to social media, from QuickBooks to Siri to weather forecasting. The magnitude of this transformation is akin to the initial wave of software applications in the 1980s and 1990s, when software first allowed for the interaction between people and computers at large scale. Machine learning will transform the way we interact with machines.

ECONOMIC IMPLICATIONS OF MACHINE LEARNING

Machine learning will affect every industry and government organization that uses software. This, of course, includes everyone. In some instances, these effects will be incremental; in others, they have the potential to be transformational.

One area where machine learning will be especially impactful is in today's transportation industry, by allowing the industry to optimize resources more effectively than ever before. For instance, imagine in the current transportation environment that we have a chaotic system of forty-passenger buses that follow fixed routes; ad hoc carpool networks that might carry a maximum of seven passengers—fifteen for someone who owns a passenger van—but are usually only partially filled; and individual drivers with three or four seats completely open in their car. Machine learning would allow for a computer system to better anticipate demand, resulting in more efficient routes and reducing the number of empty seats on the road. This results in a more effective use of existing infrastructure and can happen now. Machine learning has also made possible the upcoming self-driving car, which will see widespread use in upcoming years. Autonomous vehicles, enabled by machine-learning algorithms, will learn from each other's experience on a daily basis to build more efficient routes based on traffic and weather.

Similarly, new logistics systems—such as package and grocery delivery—that innovate to support delivery in large urban areas will be enabled by machine learning, optimizing delivery routes and systems. We will begin to see an overall optimization of integrated traffic management and transportation systems result from machine-learning-enabled computers that can process massive data sets in real time, far beyond the capabilities of city planners and distribution managers. Machine-learning systems can analyze all the process requirements and environmental characteristics within a delivery network at once, leading to a faster and far more efficient system for transporting goods.

Machine learning applied to medical science can also bring advances in modern medicine, diagnostics systems, drug research, and nutrition. Doctors will be able to leverage new models of computing to incorporate a more comprehensive, data-driven view of a patient's health into their diagnosis. Environmental factors, historical factors, patient history, family medical history, and more can be included in these algorithms to make a much more detailed projection than what a single doctor could possibly accomplish through an interview with the patient about their medical history. From a more tactile perspective, robotics is already utilized in eye surgery and will continue to advance surgical success rates, opening the door to more surgical procedures.

Even fields that are typically seen as built on the foundation of human creativity will be impacted by this catalyst. In 2016, Sci-Fi London's 48-Hour Film Challenge produced a short film titled *Sunspring* that had been authored by a recurrent neural network called long short-term memory, LSTM. Oscar Sharp, a British Academy Film Awards-nominated filmmaker, collaborated with Ross Goodwin, an AI researcher at New York University. Sharp and Goodwin named the AI bot they created to write the film Jetson, but it eventually renamed itself Benjamin. They fed Benjamin a "corpus" of sci-fi film and television scripts from the 1980s and 1990s to train him in dialogue and narrative. Benjamin then wrote the entire screenplay for *Sunspring*, including stage directions; the script was interpreted and filmed by Sharp and three actors brought on for the project. The result is an intense, strange film set in a dark future. The film also contains a song with lyrics written by Benjamin, using a database of thirty thousand folk songs fed to him by Sharp.

The film was deemed by critics a "beautiful, bizarre sci-fi comedy" and picked up for digital premiere by Ars Technica. *Sunspring* was nominated into the top ten final films at Sci-Fi London—at which point, Benjamin, the AI, assured himself a win by submitting thirty-six thousand votes per hour in the last few hours of voting.

New types of educational systems are also facilitated by machine-learning technologies as they are deployed for more personalized education experiences. This is not to say that there will no longer be human teachers, but technology can enable students to learn at their own pace according to their own individual dynamics. It is unclear exactly how this will manifest, but researchers proved long ago that different types of people learn in different ways, and optimizing an educational curriculum to fit the specific abilities and learning style of each student seems likely to lead to better educational outcomes.

Similarly, social support networks and public benefits programs could be better applied on an individualized basis, as opposed to the one-size-fits-all system. This could be possible via advanced machine-learning algorithms that are able to ingest the multitude of data points available to predict the best mix of benefits that can empower the individual or family to get back on their feet.

The rote elements of many public sector tasks, such as the filing of permits and applications, could also potentially be handled through machine-learning-enabled kiosks and online services at an office such as the Department of Motor Vehicles. Automation in these spaces could both reduce cost and enhance the constituents' experience. The same idea applies to the Internal Revenue Service, the delivery of food assistance programs, the general administration of cost-of-living equations, Medicare, and Social Security, among many others. If these calculations happened in real time rather than at the pace of bureaucracy, people would simply get the resources they need faster and more accurately.

Fire, police, emergency management, and public health systems also stand to benefit from the optimization that will be possible as a result of machine-learning-enabled technologies. To use policing as an example, many of the benefits of policing are derived from having uniformed officers on patrol in key areas at key times to deter criminal behavior. The problem has always been that we have a few officers who cover large spaces. Machine-learning tools could help with the optimal distribution of police patrols.

From a basic human perspective, these technologies bring the potential for all of us to unleash brand-new ways of being creative, tapping into the human brain in revolutionary ways. The introduction of every tool from the Stone Age forward has undoubtedly been met with the skeptical concern that it would cause humans to grow lazy, weaker, and less intelligent—or that those technologies would take away people's jobs. Hydraulics, it was thought, would keep people from working hard. Calculators would make people forget how to do long division. In reality, when new tools take on the menial tasks, the human brain is free to imagine and create in ways that would have otherwise been lost to what were previously lengthy and tedious tasks. Of course, this begs the question of what types of jobs will be lost and how the workforce will be impacted by the increasing adoption of machine-learning technology. There are real risks here, as we will discuss in greater detail when we delve into the intersection of technology and work.

JOBS THREATENED BY AUTOMATION

PROJECTED PERCENTAGE OF US JOBS AT HIGH RISK OF AUTOMATION BY 2030

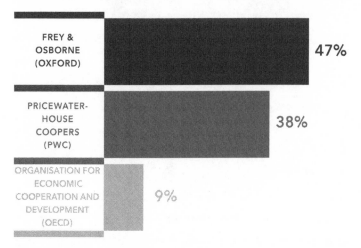

Source: Carl Benedikt Frey and Michael A. Osborne. "The Future of Employment: How Susceptible are Jobs to Computerisation?" Oxford Martin Programme on Technology and Employment, University of Oxford, Oxford, United Kingdom. September 2013.

Richard Berriman and John Hawksworth. "Will Robots Steal Our Jobs? The Potential Impact of Automation on the UK and Other Major Economies." UK Economic Outlook, PwC. March 2017.

Arntz, M., T. Gregory and U. Zierahn (2016), "The Risk of Automation for Jobs in OECD Countries: A Comparative Analysis," OECD Social, Employment and Migration Working Papers, No. 189, OECD Publishing, Paris. http://dx.doi.org/10.1787/5jlz9h56dvq7-en

Finally, when we consider job displacement and the global economy, machine-learning technologies may create similar challenges to 3D printing in developing economies. Just as 3D printing will likely reduce the need to outsource some categories of manufacturing to second and third world countries, machine learning may reduce the need to outsource some categories of services jobs. Those jobs—primarily back office and information technology services—will be among the first categories to be replaced by machine-learning-enabled software. While outsourced services are not as central to national economies as manufacturing, they are significant in many cases and serve to add a global dynamic to the issue of technology and job displacement.

GENOMICS, BIOENGINEERING, AND HEALTH TECHNOLOGY

Advances in genomics, bioengineering, and health technology have the potential to significantly enable longevity, facilitate better health longer in life, increase food supplies, and enhance human capabilities, all of which drive a multitude of second and third order effects. These developments represent a shift as significant as the development of penicillin in 1928, which served to significantly increase disease survivability and led to the creation of the pharmaceutical industry. As with the demographics and cities catalysts, developments with the potential to broadly affect how, where, and for how long people live are things we need to pay attention to. Shifts to health and longevity and human performance affect what people do, where they live, what they buy, and how they vote.

Genomics and bioengineering are related fields that comprise the study and manipulation of a human, animal, or plant's genetic material. This field has advanced significantly since the Human Genome Project, which was launched in 1990 and successfully mapped the sequence of nucleotide base pairs that make up human DNA in 2003. The Human Genome Project cost around $3 billion and took thirteen years to complete. This can now be done for less than $1,000. Illumina, an American biotechnology company, unveiled a new machine in January 2017 that it claims will reduce this cost to less than $100 and will take less than an hour.[74]

GENOMICS

NUMBER OF HUMAN GENOME BASE PAIRS SEQUENCED PER USD

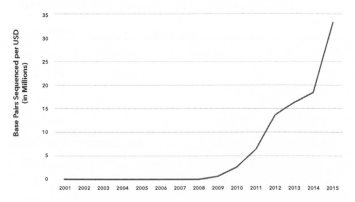

Source: Kris Wetterstrand, MS, "DNA Sequencing Costs: Data; Data from the NHGRI Genome Sequencing Program (GSP)," National Human Genome Research Institute, Genome.gov, October 31, 2017, https://www.genome.gov/27541954/dna-sequencing-costs-data/.

This is indicative of the speed at which this field is progressing. Researchers have moved past the point of focusing on understanding how genetics works, to how to manipulate genetics toward specific outcomes. There are a number of different methods, techniques, and therapies that have grown out of genomics research. While our goal is to focus on the broad implications of these technologies as opposed to the core technologies themselves, we would like to highlight one technology to provide a broad overview of what is possible.

CRISPR-Cas9 gene editing is among the most interesting of these technologies, as it allows the permanent modification of genes within living organisms. To vastly oversimplify, researchers are able to use the CRISPR-Cas9 system to effectively cut a strand of DNA at a specific location and replace it with a predesigned RNA sequence that binds to the original DNA strand (CRISPR is an abbreviation of Clustered Regularly Interspaced Short Palindromic Repeats, while Cas9 is the CRISPR associated protein). Plants and animals have both been manipulated significantly with CRISPR-Cas9 to change color, muscle tone, fur, yield, and a variety of other characteristics. This technology was first used in humans in October 2016 by Chinese scientists at the Sichuan University in Chengdu as part of a clinical trial against lung cancer.[75] American scientists used it to treat an adult mouse for muscular dystrophy in January 2016, which marked the first successful treatment of a genetic disease inside a fully developed living mammal.[76]

Again, CRISPR-Cas9 is one of many technologies in the

field of genomics and bioengineering. These technologies and techniques will provide new tools to cure disease and increasing longevity through medical treatments customized to the genome of each individual patient. Consider an antibiotic that can be tailored to the precise genome of the pathogen attacking a patient's immune system, or a cancer therapy that can seek and destroy the DNA of cancer cells specific to the patient's body. Having said this, customized medicine will be a significant challenge for the regulatory bodies of the United States and other nations with the mandate to approve drugs for use.

In the US system—regulated by the Food and Drug Administration (FDA)—a drug spends five to ten years in R&D, then another five to ten years in the trial process before being considered for FDA approval and sale. Bioengineering will shift this entire paradigm, disrupting both the pharmaceutical industry and the regulatory process overseen by government agencies. Going forward, targeted drugs could be designed for an individual's specific genetic profile, which has the potential to significantly increase the effectiveness of certain categories of drugs. In an environment of custom drugs, the paradigm where we test drugs on a small group of people in clinical trials, watch what happens, and then allow other people to take them does not make sense. Timelines are another issue, as some estimates note that it currently takes an average of twelve years and $350 million[77] to take a new drug from the laboratory to the pharmacy shelf. One could argue whether that makes sense now, but it certainly does not make sense in an environment of custom drug applications.

Genomics and bioengineering will also have deep implications in the production of food, modifying crops and livestock to increase yield and survivability in new climates. The shift from genetically enhanced foods—which we already see in GMOs—to genetically *designed* foods is the next manifestation of this trend. The ability to develop traditionally livestock-based food, such as meat, within a lab rather than on farms will drastically increase the yield and accessibility of quality protein sources around the world. Beyond the obvious benefit of being able to more cheaply feed more people, the environmental benefits of bioengineered food such as in vitro meat could be significant. Today, the largest contributor to greenhouse gas emissions comes from livestock, and in vitro meat could reduce these emissions by as much as 90 percent as well as land used to raise livestock by as much as 99 percent.[78]

As these capabilities increase the availability and decrease the cost of food, they will almost certainly contribute to a longer average human life span, as well as better health later in life, especially as they are combined with effective targeted medical therapies. This will lead to a number of significant decisions and implications for both business and public sector leaders. The most significant are the ethical considerations, which we will discuss in further detail later in this chapter. Also important is that our understanding of retirement age will need to be reevaluated, along with how we structure the eligibility requirements for a variety of social services. Companies will need to think differently about attracting, training, and enabling their workers to be productive for their companies later in life to realize the benefits of these advances.

This will also impact the types of private sector products and public sector services that will be needed for the population. There are a number of second and third order effects of increasing the average age of a population, which we covered in the demographics chapter. Products, services, transportation solutions, and living preferences are all considerations, as are the financial requirements to support retiree benefit programs, which cost more when people live longer. It is imperative that leaders in the public sector have discussions surrounding these changes and build out new frameworks for social services programs now, rather than when the world begins to see the mass impact of this catalyst. Modifying these programs will undoubtedly be difficult, but this is a key example of the forward-looking and agile leadership that is required to steward public institutions in times of transformation.

The second group of technologies related to health and

physical capabilities is the realm of health technology. By this, we specifically mean using devices on or embedded in the body to measure and enhance health and performance. There are a number of overlapping terms that constitute this emerging field. Among them are biotechnology, wearables, bioinformatics, biomanufacturing, and human-computer interfaces. An early example of embedded health technology is the artificial cardiac pacemaker; recent examples are the Fitbit and Apple Watch.

These capabilities are set to expand significantly as computing devices become smaller due to advances in chipsets, connectivity becomes more prevalent due to Internet of Things (IoT) technologies, and software becomes more capable due to the increasing integration of machine-learning algorithms. External wearables that interact with the body are already in use; you currently have a computer on your desk, on your wrist, and in your pocket. Next, there will likely be one in your bloodstream to keep you healthy and in your eye or skull to augment your ability to interact with the world.

Several of the health technologies that are emerging lead us to believe that these developments could represent a broadly relevant catalyst, as opposed to merely incremental improvements of current wearables. One area of development is embedded sensors and devices that circulate through the bloodstream, monitoring for and eventually helping to address health issues. Another is contact lenses that bring data sets directly into people's lives and workflows, enabling a new ecosystem for software application and retail experiences. A third are exoskeletons that increase performance and capability such as the Tactical Assault Light Operator Suit (TALOS), which is a robotic exoskeleton (think Iron Man) that is being developed by the US Special Operations Command.

External wearables that interact with the body are already in use; you currently have a computer on your desk, on your wrist, and in your pocket. Next, there will likely be one in your bloodstream to keep you healthy, and on your eye via glasses or contact lenses and embedded in your skull to augment your ability to interact with the world. The data extracted from this connection of body and machine will allow closer and closer interaction between biological and technological systems to improve health, productivity, and capability.

Health technology enables better health outcomes later in life, similar to genomics and bioengineering. These technologies also have the potential to enhance the capability of people in both life and work environments. This does not have to be as science-fiction sounding as a robotic exoskeleton that fights terrorists in order to be important. For example, the smartphone was a near-wearable technology that enhanced human capability. Think of the new product and software ecosystems, ways of customer interactions, and information systems that were built as a result of the smartphone. People now have computers and access to the internet on their person at all time. We view the next generation of health technology in this light, as technologies that will not only increase health outcomes but also create new platforms and product ecosystems that business and public sector leaders will need to understand and adapt to.

ETHICAL CONSIDERATIONS

While these technologies have the potential to provide tremendous benefit in terms of health, longevity, and disease prevention, they are accompanied by significant ethical considerations, some of which we as a species have never had to address. On the less complex end of this spectrum, we find concerns such as the privacy issues that come with the mainstream expansion of quantified self- and health-data technologies or the unknown health implications of eating genetically modified foods for extended periods. These are serious issues, to be certain, but they pale in comparison to the ethics of human genetic engineering.

Gene-editing technologies such as CRISPR-Cas9 are currently being designed to heal genetic-based diseases, such as sickle cell anemia. In the near future, doctors will be able to correct some of the faulty genes that lead to these ailments. This is called genome surgery, but in general, it is a procedure that does not affect germ cells, meaning that the changes to the DNA would not be passed on to future generations. With CRISPR-Cas9, germ-line engineering is possible, meaning that scientists can or will be able to make inheritable edits to human genetic code.

Alongside other developments, this leads us to an environment where the human embryo can also be edited, and those edits would be passed on to future generations. The same technology that could preemptively help avoid terrible genetic disorders such as Down syndrome and Duchenne muscular dystrophy could also potentially enable the "designer babies" scenario, where humans are engineered for increased intelligence, speed, endurance, and beauty. We are still likely between ten to twenty years away from that point, but most scientists agree that it is coming. Importantly, the history of this field leads us to believe that most tend to overestimate the time it will take to reach new technological milestones.

According to an MIT survey, 46 percent of US adults believe that changing a baby's genetic characteristics for the purpose of reducing the risk of serious diseases is appropriate.[79] Only 15 percent of the same respondents believe that it is appropriate to change a baby's genetic characteristics to make the baby more intelligent. These are significant and difficult questions to address as a society. It is also not as simple as decision by the FDA to allow or disallow this research or those procedures. This work is being done by scientists and researchers around the globe, and the ability to implement these procedures will not solely be an American decision to make. How will the public decision-making calculus change if other nations are engineering smarter and stronger children? What if these technologies are extremely expensive and thus only available to the ultrawealthy?

We do not presume to have the answers to the difficult issues, but as with other catalysts, we believe that leaders must be proactive. It is far better to understand and work to shape the emerging environment than it is to react to it after it happens. Addressing these issues in a thoughtful, comprehensive fashion will take courage. It will undoubtedly be risky for leaders who choose to do so, but the alternative—resigning leadership to technology—is akin to the tail wagging the dog.

TRENDS IN AUGMENTED REALITY

Augmented reality (AR) is the next technology that we believe has the potential for a significant impact across many different sectors. AR is often discussed in the same context as virtual reality (VR), but we see them differently and have chosen to focus our efforts on AR technologies. VR also has the potential to be extremely important and is the source of far more venture capital investment than AR, but the AR applications that impact the work, retail, and communications sectors are more intriguing to us from a broad socioeconomic perspective than the disruption that VR will bring to the entertainment industry.

AR is a hybrid visualization technology that combines the real world and the digital world. Rather than being fully immersive (i.e., a blacked-out headset where all you see are digital representations), AR systems overlay digital information onto the user's normal field of view. The technology comes in various forms: glasses, headsets, heads-up displays (HUDs) in vehicles and helmets, and in increasing volume, mobile applications and gaming.

The 2016 Pokémon GO game craze was the first true mainstream AR boom and is illustrative of how the technology works. In this game, you hold a mobile phone as you walk around real places and hunt for digital cartoon characters. When viewed on the phone, the characters appear to be live in the real-world environment. While we admit to not fully appreciating the appeal, Pokémon GO had forty-five million daily users at one point in 2016 and several hundred million installs.

Gaming is important, due to its immense popularity, and AR gaming applications will undoubtedly proliferate as a result of the recent introduction of Apple's ARKit, which opens AR app development to the wider iOS developer community; however, we are focused on the professional applications of AR technologies. Using smart glasses empowered with AR software, companies have already begun increasing the productivity and quality of skilled workers in engineering, mechanics, manufacturing, and logistics.

PROFESSIONAL AR APPLICATIONS

Upskill, a company based out of the Washington, DC, metro area, has built its business developing industry-specific AR software for smart glasses with a huge range of industry applications. Using Upskill's AR platform, end user companies can customize real-time worker enhancements for their labor forces. For instance, Boeing uses smart glasses powered by AR to guide technicians as they install wiring in planes. Once the AR-powered devices were implemented, Boeing was able to cut production time by 25 percent and lower its error rates to functionally zero. Another example is in warehouse management: GE Healthcare implemented AR software in smart glasses for its warehouse workers and immediately saw a 46 percent improvement in completing pick list order fulfillment.[80]

Just as the sensors that constitute the IoT take digital information out of the physical world, AR puts digital information back in the physical world. The fact that companies have already seen such vast improvement in worker skill, precision, and work quality in this first wave of AR-enabled industrial devices is evidence that AR will impact the workforce significantly in the decade to come. Companies have the latitude to not only think about how AR can benefit their workers within current workflows but also rethink their assumptions about worker capability. Jobs that were previously thought to be impossible can now be made possible.

AR will also change the ways that we interact with information on a personal level and the way that businesses interact with their customers. The earliest computers were based on a model of fetching data in response to commands; in order to retrieve or use the data, you were required to sit down at a terminal. This evolved into our current model of mobile and instantaneous data-fetching that we keep in our hands and pockets at all times.

AR is the next iteration in that cycle; now the information we seek will be integrated into the very environment we inhabit. Instead of looking *at* a terminal or a mobile device, we will look *through* the device and watch data interact with our world, right in front of our eyes. How would it change our interactions when we look at someone and see their LinkedIn profile, Facebook, and Twitter feeds digitally superimposed next to their faces? Or how about their criminal record? What would it mean to have the entirety of the internet packaged and visualized so that we no longer have to look up facts on Wikipedia on our phones but see them superimposed when we look at the object in question?

The retail shopping experience is another area of broad impact. In the retail space, stores can supply customers with AR-powered wearables to use as they shop. Prices, inventory, and accessory products can be automatically shown as an overlay on each item a customer picks up or looks at. IKEA has already provided customers with a tool that allows them to place furniture they are considering within an image of their living room with the touch of a button. In the home-buying market, real estate agents have created in-depth AR home tours of properties they showcase in open house events.

These technologies can also change how we interact with our work colleagues. There are a number of challenges associated with managing a dispersed workforce, but this has become a fact in the modern environment, especially for companies with multilocation or international operations. Conference call and video teleconference technology has improved significantly over the past fifteen years. While inexpensive video teleconferences have been a great addition to the corporate communications toolset, some argue that they are only of marginal benefit to the telephone and that they do not create the feeling that you are interacting with colleagues or customers in many cases.

AR and VR technologies could provide a significantly new environment for remote collaboration. Imagine looking around a conference room table and seeing digital representations of your colleagues sitting at the table with you. A manager of a remote team of employees located all over the world can virtually bring offsite team members into the meeting room, allowing for crucial interactions such as brainstorming and whiteboard planning—historically difficult to do on a conference or video call. Training employees also becomes more immersive, effective, and most importantly, expedient; complex instructions can be conveyed through a series of prompts and tutorials visible overtop the very work the employee is performing, giving "on-the-job training" a new and more precise meaning. Or imagine actually walking through a tour of a facility with an inspector or a potential client where they can see what you are seeing. The hologram avatars of science fiction could be made reality by AR and VR systems, which could finally bridge the gap between onsite and remote collaboration.

While this will drive the companies that operate video teleconference systems to make adjustments and investments in order to remain competitive, the impact could be far broader, affecting where people live and where businesses choose to operate from. As we discussed regarding transformation in cities, forces that broadly affect where and how people live are important to all companies and public sector institutions that provide products and services that are driven in part by how and where people live.

SECURITY AND PRIVACY

There are also significant applications of these technologies for military and law enforcement professionals. Imagine a world in which law enforcement has the ability to monitor populations not only with street cameras but with AR devices equipped on patrolling officers as well. Combining that with simple facial recognition—the same thing Facebook uses to automatically tag your friends— and iris scans, correct identification of persons of interest will be efficient, rapid, thorough, and accurate. Paired with machine-learning-enabled software, there is potential to identify a suicide bomber before they ever make it into a crowd and to immediately and accurately notify people in the crowd that they need to evacuate.

These systems could also vastly outperform the body camera as reliable tools to help officers provide complete real-world context behind why and how specific decisions were made in stressful situations. On the other hand, it raises questions of personal security and the role of the government. How would search and seizure rules change in this landscape? Should people in various official or even non-official roles be required to don certain types of wearables? How much information should citizens be required to share?

It is a common practice to place a red sticker in the window of a child's bedroom so that firemen know where to go first. AR for emergency responders could send them into buildings with this information already in their field of view, as well as a full blueprint of gas lines, bedrooms, and access and egress points.

The military applications for AR technology are widespread and growing fast. VR and AR are currently being used for battlefield simulation, vehicle simulation, virtual boot camp, and trauma recovery. Immersive heads-up displays will be standard issue for combat arms personnel at some point. Troops will be able to view a real-time overlay of maps, mission parameters, target identification, temperature warnings, weapon sights, topographical data—the list goes on and on. AR is much better suited for this type of environment than VR, as the transparent material of AR wearables—as opposed to occlusive and immersive VR headsets—allows the wearer to maintain situational awareness within their environment. The reality they see is *enhanced*, not virtual.

Small unit commanders could have information around

targeting, supporting weapon systems, adjacent forces, and commands overlaid on a HUD that allows for real tactical and decision-making support from anywhere in the world, without forcing an operator to stop and read a computer screen in battle. This will serve to significantly increase the precision and effectiveness of military units, allowing more and more significant operations to be conducted by smaller and smaller deployed forces.

Military vehicles will also receive the AR treatment in upcoming implementations. AR HUDs are being developed with the objective of turning tanks, planes, and ships into essentially transparent boxes, allowing the occupants to be fully immersed and aware of the environment outside the vehicle as they travel through it, while still protected by full defensive capabilities. No longer will a gunner be required to physically put his head into the turret to look around for targets; an AR headset will allow him to have a true 360-degree view of the battlefield from inside the vehicle, as opposed to merely viewing a screen as is the case now. That view will then be enhanced by target identification, friend-or-foe recognition, mapping, and other AR overlays.

BLOCKCHAIN

A fourth area within the broader category of technology that we are evaluating for significant global impact is the blockchain. Blockchain addresses the challenge inherent in digital transactions to establish trust between parties who are unknown to each other, in a way that does not require a third-party intermediary. Blockchain is a system of publicly available ledgers that keep track of who owns what. When a buyer and seller initiate a transaction, the payment processer checks the unique identifiable blockchain record to make sure that the buyer owns the element of value that is recorded on the blockchain. That exchange is then recorded in a public ledger, which is copied throughout the internet to eliminate the potential to cheat.[81]

While the blockchain and cryptocurrencies have not matured to the point where we are certain what their eventual impact will be, we are extremely sensitive to potential disruptions to the global financial system as those effects could ripple through to the global economic and geopolitical environment. It is important to note that the blockchain is not a cryptocurrency. Bitcoin is a cryptocurrency that uses blockchain technology, but for the purpose of this discussion, we are focusing on the core blockchain technology, not a specific cryptocurrency.

As blockchain provides a way to establish trust between parties, it can be used to support nearly any type of secure exchange and is not limited to a specific fiat currency or cryptocurrency. The important element for financial transactions is the idea that the blockchain eliminates the middleman. The banking and payment processing system is built on the idea that transactions need a middleman for digital purchases. Credit cards are important for credit, of course, but for the sake of this illustration, let us consider someone who has money available but uses a credit card to buy something online. In this example, credit cards reduce the risk of nonpayment for sellers—they pay the seller immediately for a transaction and then collect repayment from the buyer. In exchange for risk reduction, sellers pay credit card companies between 1–3.5 percent of every transaction.

The blockchain mechanism could significantly reduce the need for this type of intermediary. Blockchain represents a technology that could be used to validate the availability of funds and securely transfer them from the buyer's ledger to the seller's ledger in seconds to minutes. In this instance, the credit card company serving as a middleman could be displaced, saving fees for the seller, which should be reflected as lower prices to the buyer. Again, this is not to say that credit card companies are most at risk from blockchain technology, as there are many other reasons for those companies to exist and many other services that they provide for their customers. There are middlemen in other industries such as real estate, freight forwarding, investment banking, and others that receive 5–10 percent or more for ensuring transactions, who will benefit from reevaluating the long-term need for their core service.

Generally speaking, many technologies that have become mainstream in recent decades have cut out the middleman to bring buyers and sellers closer together. Uber and Lyft bring people who want rides and people who want to give rides together, without the taxi companies in between. Amazon brings manufacturers and customers closer together, eliminating the retail outlets and distribution companies in the middle. It seems likely that a similar transformation will happen in the financial services industry at some point in the next ten years. Perhaps blockchain is that technology.

Another large-scale implication is the cryptocurrencies that are built on the blockchain. There are still a great deal of development and market gyrations to occur before functioning cryptocurrencies truly emerge, but real alternates to government-issued fiat currency would have global implications. The position of international strength that the United States currently finds itself in is, in part, a result of the role of the United States at the center of the global financial system. According to the International Monetary Fund's (IMF's) currency composition of official foreign exchange reserves (COFER) data, around 64 percent of official foreign exchange reserves are denominated in the US dollar.[82] This benefits American companies because it reduces their exchange rate risk, but it also allows American monetary policy to have global importance, with political and foreign policy benefits.

A technology that disrupts banking and the transaction model will be important in its own right, but there could also be far-reaching political effects. A shift that changes the financial center of gravity away from the US dollar toward a more decentralized system would be extremely geopolitically impactful, which would have cascading effects throughout industries and companies that operate in the global marketplace.

TECHNOLOGY AND THE FUTURE OF WORK

The United States is in the midst of a generation-long structural shift in labor, productivity, jobs, and pay. This shift began in the 1980s and is set to accelerate with the increasing adoption of advanced robotics and machine-learning technologies. We are experiencing the most important changes in the nature of work since the Industrial Revolution—changes that affect nearly everything, from crime to electoral outcomes to national competitiveness.

To quote Andrew McAfee, codirector of the MIT Initiative on the Digital Economy, "Digital technologies are doing for human brainpower what the steam engine and related technologies did for human muscle power during the

Industrial Revolution."[83] Just as assumptions and fundamental behaviors that held true for agricultural societies were changed by the Industrial Revolution, assumptions and behaviors that characterized the industrial economy are being changed by the digital revolution.

The obvious outcome is that some types of jobs will go away and others will emerge. The less obvious but more important outcome is that this shift is fundamentally widening the gap between winners and losers, or those able to thrive in the digital economy and those being left behind. The workforce is bifurcating into winners and losers to a greater extent than ever before, and the dividing line is worker skill. Those with the right skills that are aligned to these emerging requirements are succeeding and accruing the benefits of the American economic engine. Those whose skills are misaligned are not participating in American economic growth and are increasingly being left behind.

Our intent is not to place a value judgment on the changing shape of labor and the economy. Structural economic forces cannot be regulated or litigated away in a free society, and they are not effectively addressed via wishful thinking. Companies and public institutions are facing a serious, potentially existential issue that will require proactive solutions. These changes are occurring and have been occurring for some time. We simply seek to explain the changes and identify where we see the trends moving.

DECOUPLING PRODUCTIVITY FROM WAGES

The first fact to acknowledge when evaluating where we are today and how we got here is that the historical correlation between labor productivity and worker wages no longer exists. This was articulated as "the great decoupling" by economists Erik Brynjolfsson and Andrew McAfee in their 2015 book *The Second Machine Age*.

Throughout the last century, labor productivity—as measured by the amount of real GDP produced by one hour of labor—continually increased as a result of technological and process-based innovation. Pay to workers—as measured by real GDP per capita, median family income, and employment—also increased in a corresponding factor. In other words, worker productivity benefited both the worker and the company.

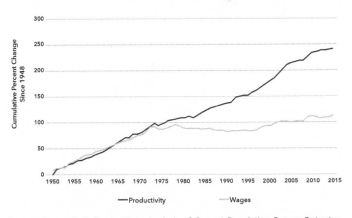

DECOUPLING PRODUCTIVITY FROM WAGES
TYPICAL WORKERS NO LONGER BENEFIT FROM NET PRODUCTIVITY GAINS

Source: Economic Policy Institute Analysis of Current Population Survey Outgoing Rotation Group Microdata, Economic Policy Institute, from "State of Working America Data Library," "Wages by Education," 2017, http://www.epi.org/data/#?subject=wage-education.

In the late 1970s and early 1980s, these values began to diverge, or decouple. Labor productivity continued to increase, but the metrics around pay and employment grew much more slowly. In the 2000s and 2010s, labor productivity continued to rise, but pay and employment flatlined and, in some cases, began to decrease. In the aggregate, the benefits of increasing worker productivity are accruing to companies and shareholders but not to the workers. In the overall context of economic productivity, work has become less valued.

INCREASING WAGE DISPARITY BASED ON SKILL

The discussion of productivity and wage data deals with aggregate trends across the United States. When we look at the wage data on a more granular basis, a stark divergence between wages and skill emerges. According to an Economic Policy Institute analysis, between 1973 and 2016 inflation-adjusted wages for individuals with advanced degrees increased by 32 percent.[84] During this same period, wages for individuals with a high school degree decreased 6 percent, and wages for those without a high school degree decreased 17 percent.

WAGE GROWTH BY EDUCATIONAL ATTAINMENT
SIGNIFICANT AND INCREASING DISPARITY IN PAY BASED ON EDUCATION

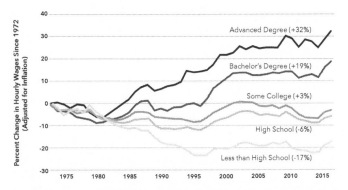

Source: Economic Policy Institute Analysis of Current Population Survey Outgoing Rotation Group Microdata, Economic Policy Institute, from "State of Working America Data Library," "Wages by Education," 2017, http://www.epi.org/data/#?subject=wage-education.

This demonstrates that, while aggregate wages have been relatively flat, the distribution of outcomes according to skill—as represented by educational attainment—is enormous and growing. The emerging digital economy has proven to be great for those with the skills and training to participate but disastrous for those without.

LABOR FORCE PARTICIPATION

At the most extreme end of the spectrum of haves and have-nots, we find those who have been utterly left behind. The most direct manifestation of being left behind is dropping out of the labor force entirely. Unemployment statistics are important to consider but do not reflect people who are not actively looking for work. Aggregate labor force participation must also be considered, and this metric depicts a sharp downturn in labor force participation in the last ten years.

Labor force participation last rose as more women entered the workforce throughout the twentieth century, then remained relatively constant from 1990 to 2008. From 2008 to 2016, the labor force participation rate dropped from 66 percent to just under 63 percent. The labor force participation rate in May 2016 was 62.6 percent, which equated to approximately 94.7 million Americans not working—near a thirty-eight-year low. When labor force participation is viewed by educational attainment or income in proportion to low education, the low-income workers who dropped out become more significant.

There are a number of different theories as to why fewer people are working. The 2008 recession was obviously a triggering event that led to a tragic number of job losses, but the lack of reentry into the workforce illustrates that this is not merely a recession issue that we should expect to rebound. Most of the hypotheses revolve around the idea that many workers who had their positions eliminated do not have the right skills to fill the new jobs that are being created and that people are opting out of a lower-income working existence because the cost of working outweighs the benefits.

Unfilled manufacturing jobs averaged 353,000 per month as of September 2016, which was almost three times the number in 2009 at the height of the recession. There were a record 5.9 million jobs available in July 2016. These are generally viewed as positive indicators for the economy, but they also raise important questions about the skills gap between jobs and job seekers.[85]

SHRINKING OF THE MIDDLE CLASS

While more people choosing to drop out of the workforce is a stark indication of the stress induced by the changing economy, it is important to note that these changes are also affecting the American middle class. The middle class is shrinking and has less relative wealth in a median sense than in the past century.

There are a number of different ways to calculate the middle class. Pew defines middle-class income as "at least two-thirds of the US median household income, but no more than double the median." According to Pew Research, the middle class shrank from 60.8 percent of Americans in 1971 to 49.9 percent in 2015, while the upper class grew from 14 percent to 21.1 percent and the lower class grew from 25.2 percent to 29 percent.[86] Again, we see evidence of growing bifurcation of outcomes between winners and losers.

The purchasing power of the middle class has also

decreased over time. Being a member of the middle class has historically meant that a family could own two cars and a house in a safe neighborhood. The US Census Bureau reports that the median household income in the country was $56,516 in 2015, which in most areas no longer supports the traditional middle-class lifestyle.

In summary, we are in the midst of a secular shift that is accruing wealth to those who have the skills to fully participate in the new economy to a greater degree than ever before. The segment of those being left behind, without the skills to participate, is also growing larger than ever before. Finally, the middle class is under pressure and shrinking relative to the upper- and lower-income segments of society.

This is a precarious labor foundation that we need to understand as we evaluate the impact of emerging advances in robotics, machine learning, and AI technology.

MACHINE LEARNING, AI, AND ROBOTICS ARE ACCELERANTS

Some new technologies—our catalysts—create new economic realities, as opposed to incremental increases to current processes and trends. The productization and broad adoption of interactive machines, enabled by machine-learning algorithms, is a catalyst that will affect every industry and public sector domain. It is unclear exactly how this will impact the labor force, but regardless of which job loss projection is correct, the trends toward the increasing social divide and bifurcation will continue. At the worst-case end of the spectrum, however, is the potential displacement of a third of the workforce and destruction of the middle class.

A plethora of forecasts predict the types and net numbers of jobs at risk of being displaced by new technologies in this domain. They range from zero—based on the assumption that job creation will equal job destruction—to 50 percent and upward—based on the assumption that every routine task and most noncreative tasks will be done by machines within the next ten years.[87]

It is important to note that displacement is not limited to low-wage jobs; a McKinsey analysis of Department of Labor data ascertained that there is only a low, statistically insignificant correlation between the average hourly wage of a job and the ability to automate that job.[88] This somewhat surprising observation leads us to the conclusion that more than the lower class is at risk. Of course, the impact on lower-income Americans is critical, as those who have already been left behind to some degree are likely to find fewer opportunities and fall even further behind in a more automated economy.

The impact on middle-income Americans represents a

potential cliff. If these technologies do offset the traditionally middle-class jobs without creating a corresponding
number of new jobs that these individuals have the skills
to perform, we could experience a dramatic collapse of
the middle class, which would have extremely negative
social and political consequences. An America in 2030
that is composed of 40 percent lower-income, 20 percent
middle-income, and 40 percent upper-income citizens
is probably not the most likely scenario, but it is within
the spectrum of possible outcomes.

BUILDING THE FUTURE WORKFORCE

This is not the first disruption to labor in this country, and
the United States has demonstrated an impressive resil-
ience in the face of prior disruption. There were thirteen
thousand businesses in the wagon and carriage industry
in 1890, according to Thomas Kinney in his book *The
Carriage Trade: Making Horse-Drawn Vehicles in America.*
And then the car came along, destroying that industry
but creating others. Some of those thirteen thousand
companies managed to transform their businesses, and
now we have reached a point where just under 750,000
Americans work as automotive service technicians and
mechanics. Another example is the bookkeeping profession, which faced an extremely difficult transition with
the advent of the personal computer and spreadsheet
software, yet accountants seem to have thrived.

We need to understand these trends and be proactive about adjusting our communities, businesses, and governments to these new realities. There is no one right answer. Business and public sector leaders must consider a number of different strategic alternatives that will result in positive outcomes. However, doing nothing or addressing these changes with wishful thinking is generally the wrong answer.

The digital revolution is a force that must be understood and worked with, not against. This is about embracing change and preparing the next generation of workers for success. If we have identified skills as the critical variable that determines whether a worker is going to be a have or have-not in this growing bifurcation of outcomes, our task is to determine how to equip people with the most relevant skills for the digital economy. This is not just a government issue; the solution does not lie in attempting to prevent change via reactionary and protectionist policies at the national level, although it will be surprising if Washington and other national governments do not try. Instead, businesses, communities, and families all must be involved in this transformation, as they stand the most to gain and lose.

The wonderful part of the digital economy is that the barriers to success for skilled workers are lower than ever before. This is not a winner-take-all environment where workers compete for a fixed number of jobs in a limited industrial base. More skilled workers create more opportunity and more economic productivity in a virtuous cycle. There is no downside to aligning the skills of workers with emerging economic requirements—it simply must be done.

TYPES OF SKILLS

Several core skills are becoming increasingly important in the digital economy. Science, technology, engineering, and mathematics (STEM) clearly provide a basis to understand and collaborate with technology, as does computer science and programming. Equally important are the types of skills that machines cannot perform. Creativity and critical thinking enable success across disciplines and are increasingly important in the digital economy. Similarly, communications and adaptability will remain in the human domain for some time.

As the pace of technological change increases, workers need the skills and flexibility to adapt and adjust over the course of their careers. The average American worker will work for twelve companies over the course of their career, with an average duration of 4.2 years per company.[89] Longevity at a company is not necessarily a good or bad thing—it is simply a reflection of the flexibility required in the digital economy that we should expect and train for going forward.

EDUCATION

The workforce of the industrial economy was hierarchical and oriented on process and efficiency. The American K–12 educational model adequately trained workers who fit the requirements of the hierarchical, process-driven, efficient workforce.

This traditional model of education needs to be reevaluated in context of the changing requirements of the digital economy. Government, education, and health care have changed the least of almost any sector over the past seventy-five years. In our schools, the teacher teaches, the students listen, performance is evaluated in a standardized one-size-fits-all fashion, and everyone takes the summer off.

Some components of the education system work well, and teaching is the single-most important profession in this country. However, we may want to rethink the education process in context of the end product of skilled citizens that it is designed to create.

HIRING AND TRAINING

Companies also need to evaluate their hiring and training processes in context of emerging worker requirements. Modern businesses survive and thrive because of human capital. Some industries have done better than others in recruiting and training talent, but this also requires a different paradigm in light of the digital economy.

From the hiring perspective, if we acknowledge that companies are rapidly iterating with new technology and business processes, the imperative is to hire workers who have the flexibility and creativity to drive these iterations. We need people who have the necessary baseline understanding of our industry but who also—and more importantly—have the skills to grow, change, communicate, and create value.

The common hiring and interview process is often inefficient at finding the type of people businesses actually need. Candidates submit résumés, and junior human resources professionals or software screen them for the required job titles and tenure. Candidates who have not been in static roles are often disqualified, when, in fact, what companies ultimately want and need is agility and flexibility. Then the interview process begins, and managers naturally seek to take the risk out of hiring by looking for individuals with demonstrated prior success. Unfortunately, this ignores the fact that success in yesterday's environment is not the same as success in tomorrow's environment.

This is a drastic oversimplification, but the hiring process at many companies has been the same for decades.

Organizations where this is the case may be well served by reevaluating this process in context of the skills they seek to bring in.

Training is another area many companies underinvest in or ignore altogether, and it affects both business performance and retention. If businesses want to hire creative, agile, critical-thinking communicators as opposed to individuals who have done the same task over and over for twenty years, they need to build a concurrent framework to train their workers and continue training them as the business and requirements evolve. The precise workers who will excel at leading growth and change within organizations will leave when they are no longer able to grow and change.

INCLUSION AND NATIONAL COMPETITIVENESS

Aligning the skills of as many people as possible to the labor requirements of the digital economy benefits everyone. It will result in happier, more-fulfilled, and better-compensated workers; lower crime; higher productive economic output; and a larger tax base.

Conversely, degrading into a bifurcated society of haves and have-nots along the skill divide benefits no one. This outcome will result in less productivity, more strife, fewer resources, and a disenfranchised majority that will change the fabric of the United States and the rest of the developed world.

National competitiveness must be addressed at the business, community, state, and national level. It transcends race, class, political ideology, age, gender, and region. Of course, these are important considerations, as some groups have more ground to make up than others. However, human talent is our most important asset, and we all benefit from getting this right.

ADAPTING WITH TECHNOLOGY

In addition to technology-based catalysts, there are also technology-based inhibitors. What does it mean if Moore's law comes to an end due to line spacing constraints, and the new phone or computer processer that comes out next year is not any faster or smaller than the one you already have? Line spacing—the distance between circuits on a microprocessor—has shrunk to 10 nanometers (nm) in current technology, as was announced in late 2017 by Samsung Electronics. Technology is coming that will provide less than 5 nm feature sizes in the next few years. This is what allows for faster and smaller computers and smartphones, but shrinking further has basic physical limitations. At some point, it may not physically be possible to run electricity through the circuit without interfering with other lines. More simply stated, there are only so many parts you can jam on a microprocessor, and we may be reaching that point.[90] How would businesses respond if the fundamental logic behind the device replacement cycle changes, and how would that affect all the suppliers and countries that source materials for consumer electronics?

We are fully aware that the developments we have highlighted in this section are only our opinion of the most important among many emerging technologies with the potential to be catalysts. There are certainly others that we did not include but could have, such as the IoT, quantum computing, space technology, nanomaterials, water technologies, and a host of other emerging developments. We have chosen to focus our discussion on areas that we see as being structurally important to everyone, everywhere. We are operating with the information that is currently available and will seek to be agile and adjust our conclusions if the data we have built our assumptions on shifts.

A prominent technologist compared machine learning and AI to the precedent of allowing sixteen-year-old teenagers to drive. When considering someone of that age, there is no possible way to predict the millions upon millions of inputs their brain will sustain, or their level and rate of experiential learning. Even so, as a society we have accepted the risks of a teenager getting behind the wheel, as long as they have passed written, behavioral, and driving tests indicating that their decisions as a driver will be reasonably safe. Without taking this measured risk, we would never be able to progress our young people forward into adult experiences. Our approach to machine learning, AI, and many of the other technologies discussed must be calculated in similar ways. It will be necessary to become comfortable with machines making decisions once we have applied testing, rigor, and standards that indicate their relative safety.

Data will increasingly become a key asset and differentiator for organizations. The more data a system has to learn from, the better it will perform, which will lead to more customers—hence, more data—in a virtuous cycle. Systems with more data perform better, which we can see when comparing Apple Maps and Google Maps. The underlying algorithms are similar, but when Apple Maps was released, it was noticeably inferior to Google Maps, who had a multiyear head start. These advantages come in all different types of businesses and can be difficult to catch up from after a slow start.

Data has always been important for companies. It is used to align product development with customer preferences and to find new customers with the same characteristics of customer bases where they have already been successful. However, we believe that data is becoming a core asset of any organization, and we encourage leaders to take a deliberate approach toward determining and structuring their basic data assets. This applies to all industries, not just the software and technology companies that most readily come to mind when we talk about data.

Consider farming, one of our oldest industries. It is responsible for most of our food, yet most outsiders to the farming industry still consider it low-tech, when in reality, the technological capabilities of today's farms make the agricultural industry one of the most high-tech industries in the world. With machine-learning algorithms applied to existing data, technology can guide farmers regarding seasons, wind, optimal places to plant, the seeds and soil that will be most prolific, and so much more. As algorithms will continue to advance, it is important to record as much data as possible in a structured format, even if the use cases are not present today.

Corporate data can also be made publicly available for social good, in what is increasingly becoming known as data philanthropy. Uber notably did this with an application called Uber Movement, making anonymized route data on more than two billion trips available to the public for free. Public transportation teams have been able to use this data to better understand the first mile and last mile gaps that public transportation does not currently fill. Other businesses have been able to use that information to innovate complementary services that work with

Uber. MasterCard and many other companies also have data philanthropy initiatives that generate goodwill from customers and enable better collaboration between the public and private sectors.

As technology advances faster and faster, it becomes more difficult, or perhaps impossible, to truly master a field. This is a challenge for business that needs to stay abreast of developments in adjacent industries, but it also applies to how we think about education and learning frameworks. One can no longer graduate from college with a knowledge base that will last for decades—the world is changing too rapidly, and there are no longer any jobs outside of the most menial labor that do not require constant adjustments. Meta-learning, or the skill of learning new skills, may be the most important tool to help ensure that we are able to evolve our skills alongside our technologies.

How do we teach ourselves and our children a framework that allows for a lifetime of continuous learning, to ensure our relevance in the face of change? It is a difficult question but one that is critical to solve.

CONCLUSION

Because this is a book, we were forced to segment our discussion on catalysts and leadership challenges into discrete chapters. In reality, there is nothing discrete about the way these forces will emerge. They will converge and interact with one another to magnify the speed and scope of change. Each of these factors would be transformational on their own. They compel significant changes that will impact the way we build our communities, do business, and live our lives. Together, they will change the foundations on which we have built our businesses and public entities. There is a remarkable amount of transformation coming as these forces converge.

This emerging environment is no longer contained in the realm of science fiction; it is becoming real more quickly than we may think. We are nearing a world in which machine-learning technology enables autonomous vehicles powered by renewables sourced on a micro-grid constantly charged via inductive charging that transport increasingly older workers to new manufacturing jobs that moved back to the United States because of additive manufacturing technology.

Across the private sector, the public sector, academia, and the nonprofit sector, leaders must wrestle with the challenges and transformations that these technologies present. How will the nature of work shift, and how do we shape our institutions and educational and hiring practices to accommodate these shifts for the benefit of our citizens and companies? How do we define and differentiate between rights and liberties in context of emerging genetic engineering technologies? What is the role of government in terms of regulations and standards with regard to these ethically, spiritually, and philosophically difficult decisions? Leaders must be proactive, open minded, and deliberate, so they can dictate the framework for these developments *before* the second and third order impacts of these developments take us by surprise.

In some cases, the convergence of these forces will reinforce their effects and make them more severe. In other cases, the mutually supportive developments will allow tools and solutions to be created that will mitigate some of the more significant challenges. Ultimately, this is a massive dance with no choreographer. There are seven billion actors from varying socioeconomic backgrounds, all looking to move forward at the same time.

There is no tidy way to conclude here, because, like you, we are not privy to the end of this story. If you have read only the chapters that might directly affect your industry, it is time to read through the rest of the book as well.

A proactive leader will want to look broadly across industries to consider how changes in other sectors interact to form new paradigms for work, productivity, community, and learning. Each new change will ripple throughout the global economy. We can consider these shifts in terms of how they affect our organizations, then begin to consider ways to seize opportunities and mitigate risks.

This is an amazing time to be alive. The increasing pace of change means we are blessed to see remarkable transformations in our lifetimes. On an individual level, we are gaining access to tools to increase knowledge, connectivity, productivity, sharing, and learning for the benefit of our communities. These opportunities only become available when we open ourselves up to them, embracing change instead of running from it and clinging to old modes of thinking.

We hope you walk away from this book with an understanding of these emerging challenges and opportunities.

Change is extremely difficult to navigate for large, successful organizations, but it is not impossible. There are models we can use and examples of success we can benefit from, but it starts with an acknowledgment of the enormity and complexity of these emerging catalysts.

By the time you read this book, there is a good chance that many of these topics will have already evolved further. Some might accelerate; others might decelerate. We spend a great deal of time researching and tracking these shifts, and we will continue to do so on a daily basis, communicating them through our various channels. We encourage you to do your own research on these catalysts, of course, but you are also welcome to leverage ours at graylinegroup.com.

The common thread through this whole story has been the human experience in all of it. Just as catalysts are change agents within the global system, people are change agents within their organizations and communities. Technologies are tools created by people, used by people, and designed to enable the success of people. Too often we focus on the technology itself but forget the human element.

Progress cannot happen without courageous people who seize the initiative to bring us collectively into the future.

Be a catalyst.

ABOUT THE AUTHORS

 **JOSEPH KOPSER** is the cofounder of the Grayline Group, a firm dedicated to the identification and management of disruptive change. Previously, he cofounded and was the CEO of RideScout. A graduate of West Point and Harvard Kennedy School, Joseph served in the US Army for twenty years.

 **BRET BOYD** is the cofounder of the Grayline Group. He is a strategy and corporate development executive with extensive experience in the defense, energy, technology, and finance sectors. A West Point graduate, Bret served in the US Special Operations Command as an infantry officer in the 75th Ranger Regiment.

NOTES

1.	"Slowing Growth Ahead for Worldwide Internet Audience," eMarketer, June 7, 2016, https://www.emarketer.com/Article/Slowing-Growth-Ahead-Worldwide-Internet-Audience/1014045.

2.	Gordon E. Moore, "Cramming More Components onto Integrated Circuits," April 19, 1965.

3.	"Metcalfe's Law," WebFinance, Inc., BusinessDictionary.com, accessed October 17, 2017, http://www.businessdictionary.com/definition/Metcalfe-s-Law.html.

4.	Mark J. Perry, "Fortune 500 Firms in 1955 v. 2015," October 12, 2015, http://www.aei.org/publication/fortune-500-firms-in-1955-vs-2015-only-12-remain-thanks-to-the-creative-destruction-that-fuels-economic-growth/.

5.	"Creative Destruction Whips through Corporate America," February 2012, https://www.innosight.com/insight/creative-destruction-whips-through-corporate-america-an-innosight-executive-briefing-on-corporate-strategy/.

6.	Robert Strohmeyer, "The 7 Worst Tech Predictions of All Time," December 31, 2008, http://www.pcworld.com/article/155984/worst_tech_predictions.html.

7.	Robert Strohmeyer, "The 7 Worst Tech Predictions of All Time," December 31, 2008, http://www.pcworld.com/article/155984/worst_tech_predictions.html.

8.	Robert Strohmeyer, "The 7 Worst Tech Predictions of All Time," December 31, 2008, http://www.pcworld.com/article/155984/worst_tech_predictions.html.

9. CBInsights. "Foot in Mouth: 37 Quotes from Big Corporate Execs Who Laughed Off Disruption When It Hit," September 2017, https://www.cbinsights.com/research/big-compay-ceos-execs-disruption-quotes.

10. Walter Isaacson, *The Innovators* (Simon & Schuster, 2014).

11. Statista, "Global Apple iPod Revenue 2006-2014," https://www.statista.com/statistics/263404/global-apple-ipod-revenue-since-first-quarter-2006/.

12. Erin Blakemore, "How Sojourner Truth Used Photography to Help End Slavery: The Groundbreaking Orator Embraced Newfangled Technology to Make Her Message Heard," SmartNews, *Smithsonian Magazine*, https://www.smithsonianmag.com/smart-news/how-sojourner-truth-used-photography-help-end-slavery-180959952/.

13. PBS, "Yellow Journalism: William Randolph Hearst," http://www.pbs.org/crucible/bio_hearst.html.

14. Joseph Schumpeter, *Capitalism, Socialism, and Democracy,* 1942.

15. Jason Dempsey, "Our Generals Failed in Afghanistan," *Stars and Stripes,* October 2016, https://www.stripes.com/opinion/our-generals-failed-in-afghanistan-1.434716.

16. Mark J. Perry, "Fortune 500 Firms 1955 vs. 2016," AEIdeas, December 2016, http://www.aei.org/publication/fortune-500-firms-1955-v-2016-only-12-remain-thanks-to-the-creative-destruction-that-fuels-economic-prosperity/.

17. Lily Hay Newman, "Google is Moving Away From its Original Mission Statement," November 3, 2014, http://www.slate.com/blogs/future_tense/2014/11/03/larry_page_says_that_google_needs_to_move_on_from_its_don_t_be_evil_mission.html.

18. Rebecca M. Henderson, and Ryan Johnson, "Nestle SA: Nutrition, Health and Wellness Strategy," Harvard Business School Case (June 2011; Revised May 2012): 311-119, https://hbr.org/product/Nestl%C3%A9-SA--Nutrition--Hea/an/311119-PDF-ENG.

19. "An Overview of 60 Contracts That Contributed to the Development and Operation of the Federal Marketplace," Department of Health and Human Services, August 2014, https://oig.hhs.gov/oei/reports/oei-03-14-00231.pdf.

20. Jack Stewart, "America Gets a D Plus for Infrastructure," Wired, March 2017, https://www.wired.com/2017/03/america-gets-d-plus-infrastructure-big-bill-fix/.

21. Christensen, Clayton. *The Innovator's Dilemma*. USA, Harvard Business Review Press, 1997.

22. Jacob Fader, "15 Corporate Accelerators Giving Startups a Boost," TechCo, August 15, 2017, https://tech.co/corporate-accelerators-startups-2017-08.

23. In-Q-Tel. https://www.iqt.org/.

24. Alex Larzelere, "Transforming Insight: Corporate Near Death Experiences," Grayline, March 28, 2017, https://graylinegroup.com/transforming-insight-corporate-near-death-experiences/.

25. Alex Larzelere, "Transforming Insight: Corporate Near Death Experiences," Grayline, March 28, 2017, https://graylinegroup.com/transforming-insight-corporate-near-death-experiences/.

26. Jonathan Coopersmith, *Faxed: The Rise and Fall of the Fax Machine* (JHU Press), 2015.

27. Tom March, *Laptop Global Supply Chain,* http://tommarch.com/2010/06/laptop-global-supply-chain/.

28. Wohlers Associates, "Wohlers Report 2017: 3D Printing and Additive Manufacturing State of the Industry Annual Worldwide Progress Report."

29. "The State of 3D Printing," Sculpteo, April 2015, http://www.sculpteo.com/static/0.30.0-64/download/report/Sculpteo_State_of_3D_Printing.pdf.

30. UPS, "3D Printing: The Next Revolution in Industrial Manufacturing," https://pressroom.ups.com/mobile0c9a66/assets/pdf/pressroom/infographic/UPS_3D_Printing_executive%20summary.pdf.

31. Rose George, *Ninety Percent of Everything: Inside Shipping, the Invisible Industry That Puts Clothes on Your Back, Gas in Your Car, and Food on Your Plate* (Picador), 2014.

32. Danit Peleg, "3D Printed Fashion: Your Own 3D Printed Jacket," Danit Peleg, https://danitpeleg.com/.

33. "Review of the Maritime Transport 2015," United Nations Conference of Trade and Development, United Nations (2015): 7, http://unctad.org/en/PublicationsLibrary/rmt2015_en.pdf.

34. Reuters, "Hanjin Is Scrambling to Move about $14 Billion in Stranded Cargo," *Fortune*, September 8, 2016, http://fortune.com/2016/09/08/hanjin-shipping-funding-stranded-cargo/.

35. Barrett Tillman, *D-Day Encyclopedia: Everything You Want to Know About the Normandy Invasion*, World War II Collection (Regnary History), 2014.

36. "Renewable Infrastructure Investment Handbook: A Guide for Institutional Investors," World Economic Forum, December 2016, http://www3.weforum.org/docs/ WEF_Renewable_Infrastructure_Investment_Handbook.pdf.

37. "Use of Energy in the United States Explained," US Energy Information Administration, May 17, 2017, https://www.eia.gov/Energyexplained/?page=us_energy_transportation.

38. Zachary Shahan, "California Now Has 1 Gigawatt of Solar Power Installed," Clean Technica, November 11, 2011, https://cleantechnica.com/2011/11/11/california-now-has-1-gigawatt-of-solar-power-installed/.

39. David Feldman, Galen Barbose, Robert Largolis, Ted James, Samantha Weaver, Naim Darghouth, Ran Fu, Carolyn Davidson, Sam Booth, and Ryan Wiser, "Photovoltaic System Pricing Trends," SunShot, US Department of Energy, NREL.gov, September 22, 2014, https://www.nrel.gov/docs/fy14osti/62558.pdf.

40. Sara Matasci, "How Solar Panel Cost and Efficiency Have Changed Over Time," Energy Sage, March 16, 2017, http://news.energysage.com/solar-panel-efficiency-cost-over-time/.

41. "2017 US Energy and Employment Report," Energy.gov, accessed January 22, 2018, https://www.energy.gov/downloads/2017-us-energy-and-employment-report.

42. Morgan Lyons, "Solar Industry Sees Largest Quarter Ever," Seia.com, December 14, 2016, https://www.seia.org/blog/solar-industry-sees-largest-quarter-ever#.

43. Solar Roof, Tesla, accessed January 22, 2018, https://www.tesla.com/solarroof.

44. Global Wind Energy Council, Global Wind Statistics 2015. Published October 2, 2016.

45. "Wind Generation Output Tops 15,000 MW in ERCOT Region," ERCOT, November 28, 2016, http://www.ercot.com/news/releases/show/113533.

46. Jan Dell and Matthew Klippenstein, "Wind Power Could Blow Past Hydro's Capacity Factor by 2020," Greentech Media, February 2017, https://www.greentechmedia.com/articles/read/wind-power-could-blow-past-hydros-capacity-factor-by-2020.

47. "Electrifying Insights," McKinsey & Company, Advanced Industries, January 2017, https://www.mckinsey.de/files/161223_mckinsey_e-vehicles.pdf.

48. Fred Lambert, "Tesla Confirms Base Model 3 Will Have Less Than 60 kWh Battery Pack Option, Cost Is below $190/kWh and Falling," electrek, April 26, 2016, https://electrek.co/2016/04/26/tesla-model-3-battery-pack-cost-kwh/.

49. "Renewable Energy Country Attractiveness Index," EY, accessed January 22, 2018, http://www.ey.com/gl/en/industries/power---utilities/renewable-energy-country-attractiveness-index.

50. "A Cheap, Long-Lasting, Sustainable Battery for Grid Energy Storage: Oh, and They Don't Explode," Kurzweil Accelerating Intelligence, September 2, 2016, http://www.kurzweilai.net/a-cheap-long-lasting-sustainable-battery-for-grid-energy-storage.

51. "Short-Term Energy Outlook," US Energy Information Administration, December 2017, https://www.eia.gov/outlooks/steo/report/global_oil.cfm.

52. "Review of Maritime Transport," UNCTAD, 2015, http://unctad.org/en/PublicationsLibrary/rmt2015_en.pdf.

53. Stephen G. Benka, "The Energy Challenge," *Physics Today* 55:4 (2002): 38-39.

54. "Solar Paint Offers Endless Energy from Water Vapour." RMIT University, June 2017, https://www.rmit.edu.au/news/all-news/2017/jun/solar-paint-offers-endless-energy-from-water-vapour.

55. United Nations, Department of Economic and Social Affairs, Population Division (2015), World Population Prospects: The 2015 Revision, DVD Edition.

56. Wolfgang Lutz and Sergei Scherbov, "Exploratory Extension of IIASA's World Population Projections: Scenarios to 2300," IIASA, http://webarchive.iiasa.ac.at/Admin/PUB/Documents/IR-08-022.pdf.

57. "The Future of World Religions: Population Growth Projections, 2010–2050," Pew Research Center, April 2, 2015, http://www.pewforum.org/2015/04/02/religious-projections-2010-2050/.

58. "Europe Needs Many More Babies to Avert a Population Disaster," *The Observer*, August 2015, https://www.theguardian.com/world/2015/aug/23/baby-crisis-europe-brink-depopulation-disaster.

59. Phillip Connor and C'Vera Cohn, "Changing Patterns of Global Migration and Remittances," Pew Research Center, December 2013, http://www.pewsocialtrends.org/2013/12/17/changing-patterns-of-global-migration-and-remittances/.

60. "Modern Immigration Wave Brings 59 Million to US, Driving Population Growth and Change Through 2065," Pew Research Center, September 28, 2015, http://www.pewhispanic.org/2015/09/28/modern-immigration-wave-brings-59-million-to-u-s-driving-population-growth-and-change-through-2065/.

61. Allison Smale, "A Booming Germany Woos Immigrants," *The New York Times*, July 2104, https://www.nytimes.com/2014/07/19/world/europe/needing-skilled-workers-a-booming-germany-woos-immigrants.html.

62. Gary Marshall, "Robot Chores: The Droids Are Coming for Your Job, and No One's Safe," Tech Radar, August 20, 2016, http://www.techradar.com/news/world-of-tech/robot-chores-the-droids-are-coming-for-your-job-and-no-one-s-safe-1326824.

63. Automated Insights, https://automatedinsights.com/case-studies/associated-press.

64. Adam Pasick. "Sales of adult diapers to surpass baby diapers in aging Japan." *Nikkei*. https://qz.com/103000/sales-of-adult-diapers-surpass-baby-diapers-in-aging-japan/.

65. United Nations, Department of Economic and Social Affairs, Population Division (2015), World Population Prospects: The 2015 Revision, DVD Edition.

66. James Manyika, "Urban America: US Cities in the Global Economy," *McKinsey*, April 2012, http://www.mckinsey.com/global-themes/urbanization/us-cities-in-the-global-economy.

67. Karen C. Seto, Burak Güneralp, and Lucy R. Hutyra. B.L. Turner, ed. "Global forecasts of urban expansion to 2030 and direct impacts on biodiversity and carbon pools." Yale School of Forestry and Environmental Studies, New Haven, CT; Department of Geography, Texas A&M University, College Station, TX; and Department of Geography and Environment, Boston University, Boston, MA. August 2012.

68. Lucy Wescott, "More Americans Moving to Cities, Reversing the Suburban Exodus," *The Atlantic*, March 27, 2014, https://www.theatlantic.com/national/archive/2014/03/more-americans-moving-to-cities-reversing-the-suburban-exodus/359714/.

69. Lydia Epp Schmidt, "5 World Record Apartments," Naked Apartments, September 12, 2014, https://www.nakedapartments.com/blog/5-world-record-apartments/.

70. Sarah Halzack, "Walmart Is Ending Its Express Concept and Closing 269 Stores," *The Washington Post*, January 15, 2016, https://www.washingtonpost.com/news/business/wp/2016/01/15/walmart-is-ending-its-express-concept-and-closing-269-stores.

71. Amy Nordrum, "Popular Internet of Things Forecast of 50 Billion Devices by 2020," IEEE Spectrum, August 2016, https://spectrum.ieee.org/tech-talk/telecom/internet/popular-internet-of-things-forecast-of-50-billion-devices-by-2020-is-outdated.

72. "Segregated City," Martin Prosperity Institute, http://martinprosperity.org/media/Segregated%20City.pdf.

73. Hassan Mujtaba, "Intel 14nm Broadwell-EP Family Launched—Xeon E5-2600 V4 For Next-Gen Workstation Platforms With 7.2 Billion Transistors," wccftech.com, March 31, 2016, https://wccftech.com/intel-broadwell-ep-xeon-e5-v4/.

74. Sara Buhr, "Illumina Wants to Sequence Your Whole Genome for $100," *TechCrunch,* https://techcrunch.com/2017/01/10/illumina-wants-to-sequence-your-whole-genome-for-100/.

75. Fiona McDonald, Science Alert, November 2016, https://www.sciencealert.com/crispr-gene-editing-has-been-tested-in-a-human-for-the-first-time.

76. Peter Dockrill, Science Alert, January 2016, https://www.sciencealert.com/crispr-gene-editing-tool-used-to-treat-genetic-disease-in-an-animal-for-the-first-time.

77. "New Drug Approval Process," Drugs.com, https://www.drugs.com/fda-approval-process.html.

78. Kristin Houser, "Lab-Grown Meat Is Healthier; It's Cheaper, It's the Future," Futurism, February 2017, https://futurism.com/were-5-years-away-from-lab-grown-meat-hitting-store-shelves/.

79. Antonio Regalado, "Engineering the Perfect Baby," MIT Technology Review, March 2015, https://www.technologyreview.com/s/535661/engineering-the-perfect-baby/.

80. "Augmented Reality Uses Cases in Enterprise," Upskill, https://upskill.io/skylight/use-cases/.

81. Alex Larzelere, "Blockchaining the World," Grayline, April 1, 2017, https://graylinegroup.com/blockchaining-the-world/.

82. "Currency Composition of Official Foreign Exchange Reserves," IMF, http://data.imf.org/.

83. Amy Bernstein and Anand Raman, "The Great Decoupling: An Interview with Erik Brynjolfsson and Andrew McAfee," *Harvard Business Review* (June 2015), https://hbr.org/2015/06/the-great-decoupling.

84. Economic Policy Institute Analysis of Current Population Survey Outgoing Rotation Group Microdata, Economic Policy Institute, from "State of Working America Data Library," "Wages by Education," 2017, http://www.epi.org/data/#?subject=wage-education.

85. United States Bureau of Labor Statistics (BLS), https://www.bls.gov/data/.

86. "The American Middle Class Is Losing Ground," Pew Research Center, December 9, 2015, http://www.pewsocialtrends.org/2015/12/09/the-american-middle-class-is-losing-ground/.

87. Benedikt Frey, and Michael A. Osborne, "The Future of Employment: How Susceptible Are Jobs to Computerisation?" *Oxford University*, September 2013.

88. Michael Chui, James Manyika, and Mehdi Miremadi, "Four Fundamentals of Workplace Automation," McKinsey & Company, McKinsey Quarterly, November 2015, https://www.mckinsey.com/business-functions/digital-mckinsey/our-insights/four-fundamentals-of-workplace-automation.

89. Quentin Fottrell, "Typical US Worker Has Been 4.2 Years in Their Current Job," Market Watch, January 12, 2014, https://www.marketwatch.com/story/americans-less-likely-to-change-jobs-now-than-in-1980s-2014-01-10.

90. Alex Larzelere, "Microprocessors and Line spacing: The End of an Era," Grayline, June 21, 2017, https://graylinegroup.com/microprocessors-line-spacing-end-era/.